HOW TO GET A DATE WITH A VAMPIRE

How to Get a Date with a Vampire

(And What to Do with Him Once You've Got Him)

KIKI OLSON

CB

CONTEMPORARY
BOOKS

CHICAGO

Library of Congress Cataloging-in-Publication Data

Olson, Kiki.
How to get a date with a vampire : and what to do with
him once you've got him / Kiki Olson.
p. cm.
ISBN 0-8092-3843-8 (paper)
1. Vampires—Humor. I. Title.
PN6231.V27044 1992
646.7′7—dc20 92-18519
CIP

Published by Contemporary Books, Inc.
180 North Michigan Avenue, Chicago, Illinois 60601
Manufactured in the United States of America
International Standard Book Number: 0-8092-3843-8

CONTENTS

INTRODUCTION: WHY VAMPIRES MAKE BETTER BOYFRIENDS

 Ever since Bela Lugosi uttered those fateful words, "look into my eyes," women everywhere have been enraptured by these creatures of the night. What *is* it about these guys that compels us to devour Anne Rice's novels, scour *TV Guide* for "Dark Shadows" reruns, and flock to the movies to see actors such as Frank Langella, David Bowie, and, yes, even George Hamilton portray "the man in the evening clothes who longs for the most forbidden love of all"?

Certainly it's not that we're in love with those corny old come-ons (besides, we *never* fall for them, do we, ladies?), although I must admit that when a vampire seductively asks, "haven't we met before," I kind of get the feeling that he *believes* it—either that, or he's confusing me with Venus, the goddess of love (*quelle tragédie!*). So what, what, *what* is it? Could it be our fascination with the geopolitics of Romania? Our admiration for *any* man who understands the beauty of a well-preserved cobweb? Our unbridled envy of a lifestyle that precludes getting out of bed before dinnertime?

Not on your life! It's because vampires are *sexy*. They know how to dress. They know what to say. They're hopelessly romantic and they're passionately sincere. They're moody, mysterious, dangerous, and unapologetic. They're the bad boys our mothers warned us against, and my oh my are they fun. Best of all, *they know how to make a commitment*. Vampires are everything, in fact, a woman could want in a man—and more.

The trick is getting a date with one.

The good news, darlings, is that dating the damned doesn't have to be just a late-night fantasy. Vampires are everywhere, if you know where to look, and they are yours for the taking, if you know what to do. It's just like any big date—in order for it to work, *you have to be prepared*. It's also a good idea, I think, to know what you're getting into with these guys. After all, it's one thing to lust after your toothsome Romeo from afar—say, from the comfy confines of the back row of your local Cineplex. But where do you turn for advice when it's time to introduce your vamparamour to your parents? How do you handle his obsession with his former girlfriends? (Remember, you really *could* be competing against Venus, or at least some mortal love goddess like Cleopatra here!) Just how far should a girl stick her neck out on the first date, and how can you tell if he's Mr. Perfect Teeth or just another hound dog from hell?

That's why I've written this book. You see, I've been dating these guys for *years*, and believe me, I've learned a thing or two about them. Just as with any mortal man, there are tricks to relationships with vampires. There are also traps. Yes, dating these devils can be the dream come true of a lifetime (no matter how brief that lifetime may turn out to be), but it's not all moonlight and blood-red roses. On the contrary—if I had a ruble for every drop of blood I've spilled over these heartbreakers, I'd own my own Transylvanian castle! The truth is vampires can be the most difficult, most exasperating, most *exhausting* men in the world. But you know what? They're worth it, because they know how to make a woman feel more special, more *female*, than any other man ever has or ever will again. And that to me (and I'll bet to you too) is worth all the sunrises in the universe.

So, by all means, use my experience with these divine creatures and snare the man of *your* dreams. Read this book, and you too will have all the know-how you need to *really* sink your teeth into a romance with a vampire. As the ad says, ''live the fantasy.'' Well, heck, why not?

✣ 1 ✣
How to Spot a Vampire

"Vampires are generally described as dark, sinister-looking, and singularly handsome. Our Vampire was, on the contrary, rather fair. . . ."

So wrote Stanislaus Eric, Count Stenbock, in "The Sad Story of a Vampire" in 1894. See, even back then, those in the know where aware that the image of a vampire as the hollow-eyed ooky guy in the black cape and funny accent was a silly stereotype. *Real* vampires come in every age group, body type, and ethnic and religious persuasion. (I personally have found more than my share of the Irish variety. But there may be a good reason for that. Bram Stoker, the author of *Dracula*, was a Dubliner.)

Vampires don't have to look and act like bad boy extraordinaire Mickey Rourke did in the modern vampire movie *9½ Weeks* either (well, of course they never came out and *said* he was a vampire, but we know better, don't we?). They can appear as innocently innocuous as Tom Cruise, Michael Jordan (that's *Jordan*, not Jackson), or Warren Beatty (although it seems old Warren can't hide it anymore, can he?).

Another vampire myth is that these guys lie around all day and expose themselves only at night, when they leave their graves to spend their active hours sucking blood from the necks of mesmerized victims. What nonsense! While the "exposing themselves at night" and "mesmerized victims" parts have a ring of truth, vampires *don't* have to get a regular transfusion to make it to the dawn. Some vampires have reached such a high level of sophistication that they can go for centuries without even a demitasse of type B. This is not to say they won't leave the women in their lives in a state of mental and physical exhaustion. They will. They just don't have to draw blood to do it.

Yet another bit of vampire fluff is that he can assume the form of a bat whenever he feels like it. This is because there is an animal called a vampire bat. The little critter thrives on blood, which it obtains by piercing its victim's flesh with its two sharp front teeth. Sounds familiar, I know. But the bat preys on cattle. Our vampires may have a sexual quirk or two (thank heavens!), but they do draw the line at farm animals.

Although there's no documented proof that blood type matters to a vampire, I have long felt that my being born under the sign of O positive (The Universal Giver) has put me in a unique position to intimately get to know a wide range of vampire guys from all over the world and from all walks of life. As a result of these experiences, I've been able to figure out almost from the get-go whether a new man in my life is a vampire or not. Here's my home-grown method: Say I meet a man at a dinner party. I register that he is attractive, amusing, and bright. Any man can fill that bill, right? *But*, it's only if, after we've had a chat and he's promised to call and possibly even gone so far as to give me a peck on the cheek, I begin to feel the gray-green swoon of carsickness sweep over me that I *know* I've met a vampire!

By and large, carsickness is a fairly accurate description of the malady a vampire leaves you with. It has to do with something we vampire groupies call the Mesmerization Factor (MF). Think about it—if your stomach fills up with butterflies at just the mention of the word *vampire*, what effect do you think his actual lips on your blood-flushed cheek can produce? That's right—a feeling not a little like descending a twisty, turny road with million-mile-deep crevasses on either side of you. "Danger, danger!" your brain cries out, but does your heart care one whit about that? Absolutely not, and who can blame it, when it's pumping madly, full of reckless abandon and overwhelmed by the thrill of the ride? You've been mesmerized with a capital *M*. You are his.

As a medical colleague of mine who has researched trauma in vampire victims explains, "Unlike an illness such as the flu where you can take an antibiotic, or a gash that an emergency ward can stitch up, or food poisoning that can be tossed up and forgotten, terminal carsickness is the state in which the vampire usually leaves his prey. She is powerless to do anything. She loses her interest in reading, eating, sleeping, working—in everything but him. Pretty soon her brain becomes so numb she can't even figure out that if she could pull herself together to the point of getting some sunshine, she might get over it." (But who *wants* to get over it, I say.)

Most women have to develop their own feelers for scoping out the vampires who stumble into their lives (Marta, a friend of mine, claims, "Anytime I meet a guy and he makes me feel like a fly trapped in amber just by smiling at me, I know I'm in Vampire City."), but here are some hard and fast rules that have been used successfully for centuries.

▼ *1. Does he appear to be in need of some ortho work*, particularly in the pearly canine department? Fangs are a dead giveaway. Of course, vampires who have been "reborn" into affluent families (somehow George Hamilton springs to mind again) may have had the advantage of getting extensive orthodontic work early on. This clue then becomes invalid. Another rule of thumb, then, is this: if his smile is *too* perfect and his choppers look like a Chiclets convention, chances are he's bought into bonding to cover up a menacing overbite and he *is* a vampire.

▾ *2. Does he have a nickname? Does he use several names?* Vampires rarely have straightforward names like Herb or Sam that they use day in and day out. This goes back to the original vampire guys. Both father (Dracul) and son (Dracula) had the given name Vlad. The names Dracul and Dracula are really nicknames. Daddy Dracul's pet name had two meanings in Romanian—"little devil" or "little dragon." Young Dracula picked another nickname for himself. He called himself Vlad Tepes, which meant "Vlad the Impaler." (Talk about *macho*—this guy must really have been full of himself. But then, most vampires are.) Anyway, that's how the nickname phenomenon began. It's a good bet that modern vampire nicknames such as, oh, Arsenio, probably mean "little arsonist" in Romanian (or, in the English translation, "light your fire"—listen, vampires are *nothing* if not sure of themselves!).

Another good clue is the "more-than-one-name" appellation. Next time you're on the prowl for a vampire, look for guys who have *two* first names that they use as a full name—like Billy Dee Williams. (Or even Robin Williams.) They've probably dropped their *real* last names because they don't want the world to know they're part of the Prince of Wallachia bloodline.

Due to their complex character, vampires will often introduce themselves to different people using a *variety* of names. Is it because of their secretive nature? Their picaresque sense of humor? Their innate need to muddy the waters? Since you'll never know, just remember, when the most attractive man in the room is alternately called Orville, Raimondo, Eli, and Pierre, you can put money on his being a vampire.

▼ *3. Find out who his friends are.* Or, I should say, *friend.* Ever since Dracula first made his appearance on the silver screen, he has had a faithful servant/buddy known as Renfield. So do modern vampires, except now Ren will sport a regular name like Dave, Ralph, or Harry. A Renfield is a very ordinary mortal. When a vampire introduces him to you, you'll probably ask yourself, "What could that fantastic man and this dweeb have in common?" Very little, except need. The Renster exists to make the vampire look even *more* fantastic by comparison. He's also around to pick up the vampire's shirts from the laundry, run to the bank, and perform all those other chores that can be accomplished only during daylight hours. He's the designated driver who takes the vampire to evening soccer games and the pub crawl afterward. He's there to keep you, the vampire's date, company for hours on end while your Romanian Romeo gets his beauty sleep. And, should the day—or night—come when your vampire leaves you high and dry for that exotic damsel with the fiery B-negative blood, it's Renfield who gets to deliver the "you're a nice girl, but you just weren't his *type*" bailout line. Be nice to him.

▼ *4. Does he vehemently avoid restaurants where he knows many of the dishes are flavored with garlic?* In olden days, any person who didn't eat garlic was suspected of being a vampire. For many of us, that's still the case today, but recent anthropological findings in Transylvania have proved that the reason behind this culinary quirk is not that, as was once believed, vampires *fear* garlic. Vampires, it turns out, enjoy *nothing more* than snails swimming in garlic butter, tangy pesto on their angel hair pasta, and a nice New Orleans–style muffaletta. Because a vampire is so consummately romantic, however, he realizes that if he consumes a garlic-enhanced meal before getting down to the evening's main course (that's you), he'll have to use some minty concoction to render his breath French-kissing sweet. *And vampires can't tolerate the taste of mint.* It's that simple!

▼ *5. Does he tend to disappear right before a group picture is about to be taken?* Does he walk past mirrors so quickly you never get to see his image in one? Let's put another old wives' tale to bed. That is, "a vampire's image does not reflect, and therefore, cannot be seen in a photograph or a mirror." Stuff and nonsense! Actually, vampires do tend to shun self-reflection, but that's not why they shy away from photo booths. Vampires avoid having their pictures taken simply because they are generally wanted in several states, or because they are considerate enough to not want their many wives to see where they've been. They don't look in mirrors because *they don't have to.* They can see how wonderful they are just by looking into the adoring eyes of the women surrounding them. (That's why vampires are always using that "look into my eyes" line. All the better to see *themselves*, my dears!)

▼ *6. Do his eyes seem to follow you around the room? Even if he's been sitting or standing in one spot?* Vampires— even those wearing sunglasses (remember Jason Patric in *The Lost Boys*?) can speak volumes with their eyes and can make the most casual glance as seductive as a tango (which happens to be one of their favorite ballroom dances). A vampire's hypnotic stare is no accident, my dears. It's the result of having spent years studying with ritual hypnotist Franz Mesmer so he can mesmerize a woman across a crowded room. Dr. Mesmer also thought up the theory of animal magnetism—something the vampire has elevated to an art form. Once you're under his spell—and it won't take long—he'll have you barking at the moon, riding with the hounds, and performing any stupid animal trick he finds amusing. And you won't even know it's happening!

▼ *7. After having a deep, meaningful conversation with him, do you find yourself thinking*, "What an incredible guy. I've got to know *more* about him!" The reason you feel that way is because, although he may have sweet-talked you for hours, he hasn't really said anything about himself at all. The vampire is such a brilliant conversationalist, he's able to ramble on *forever* without giving you a clue about where he's been and where he's going. If there were a one-word limit on defining a vampire, it would be "vague." But be warned. There is also a breed of vampire who will be blindingly precise. He will let you in on the hour of his birth, the middle names of each of his nieces and nephews, and his grades in graduate school as well as anecdotes about his childhood friends and current coworkers. In short, after spending a couple of hours with this guy you'll feel that you know *everything* about him. It will take a while before you realize he's made it all up.

♥ *8. Is the most appealing guy at the Halloween party wearing a Dracula suit?* That's because he might very well *be* a vampire. Or maybe you just *wish* he were the real McCoy—it could go either way. When in doubt, use the carsick test. Feeling swoony? Bingo! He's *It*.

Before you get too cocky and think you can spot a vampire from a mile away, let's make it clear that there are no standard models. A vampire can be a Danny Glover look-alike car salesman from New Jersey, a rock star of the Eric Clapton genre, or a California heart surgeon with a Mel Gibson grin.

Trust me—once you master the tricks for spotting them, you'll see that *vampires are everywhere*. And, like a mass of eager-to-please ectoplasm waiting for the seance to begin, once you send out the signals to summon yours, he *will* appear.

❧ 2 ❧
THE PROFESSIONAL VAMPIRE

Movies, plays, and books usually portray vampires as sleeping around all day (which *can* be the case), then haunting castles all through the night, dressed to the nines, and generally living (so to speak) off the fat of the land. Nothing could be further from the truth! Although there are vampires who do elect to become playboys and welfare recipients, the majority prefer to enter a variety of fascinating, responsible, well-paying fields. Really, after a century or two of playing the carefree bon vivant, a vampire can get a bit bored. But don't think he'll take just *any* job that happens to offer a graveyard shift.

Since he possesses an independent, somewhat intractable nature, a vampire is not cut out to be a nine-to-five (even P.M. to A.M.) company man, toiling away at someone else's business, expecting a gold watch and modest pension come retirement. Retirement, after all, has never been one of the vampire's options.

You won't find a vampire involved in "cliché" professions like undertaking, archaeology, and taxidermy either. The dead hold no particular professional interest for him. He already knows all about that world.

He'll also give short shrift to construction work. This is not because he minds getting his hands dirty— it's just that the idea of *con*struction is alien to him. *Des*truction is more the ticket.

In the last couple of centuries, the medical profession has attracted vampires in droves—dentistry in particular. The reason is obvious. It's the ortho work they need for their fangs, and because they are such perfectionists, vampires are unwilling to have anyone else design their precious choppers.

My first experience with a vampire dentist occurred some years ago. I was at a trattoria trying to suck out the last bit of marrow from a tasty *osso buco milanese*. In the process, I cracked one of my caps—a front one, so smiling my way out of that humiliating situation was out of the question. My regular dentist had just retired to some Central American tax haven, so I was forced to call an emergency dental referral service, who told me Dr. X was just a few blocks away and could see me in 12 minutes. (Because of either an elliptical sense of time or a basic perverseness, vampires choose not to make regular appointments like "see you at noon, 7:30, 3:00," etc. They prefer more helter-skelter times like 11:26, 2:47, or 9:58. You get used to it after a while.)

At exactly 8:42 P.M. I walked into his office. The minute I saw him, I sensed he'd been working on molars since at least the Inquisition! He was tall, dark, and handsome. (When was the last time you saw a *human* dentist who fit that description?) Neatly unclenching a welcoming grin, he bade me come in and invited me to make myself at home. Unlike the spare, steely dentist offices I'd been drilled at before, his was flatteringly lit, with excellent examples of Middle European art on the walls. Even his dentist's chair was cozy. Did I mention that instead of wearing hospital greens or white, he had on a midnight black, pure silk tuxedo, complete with a dazzling floor-length cape? (He did mention something about going to the theater later. *Oh, sure,* I thought.) Anyway, it took him but a few painless moments to put my mouth back together so I was able to get back to the restaurant in time for *zuppa inglese* and espresso.

As of that night, Dr. X has been my permanent Tooth Guardian. Let me tell you, dentistry is definitely one profession where the old MF (Mesmerization Factor) comes in quite handy. I'm always far too hypnotized by his penetrating eyes to be bothered with using novocaine, which makes me feel like I'm carrying a soggy tennis ball in my mouth all day anyway. One night after a routine checkup, I *jokingly* asked him if the D.M.D. after his name stood for "Don't Mind Dracula." "Don't *Mock* Dracula," he responded, giving me all the glitter of his toothsome grin.

Anyway, on to other professions. Medical schools have graduated many a vampire, but don't jump to the conclusion that it's because they see becoming a doctor as the easiest way to get close to the plasma. Rather than choosing careers as battle surgeons, vampires are far more likely to enter medicine's more delicate arenas—like that of plastic surgery. The vampire, you see, prefers a "change" to a "cure." Psychiatry is another favored specialty. It allows the vampire to sit in a position of ultimate control—something, you'll find, he needs far more than a shot of Rh-negative.

Because it attracts born exhibitionists who love the nightlife, show business is an obvious magnet for vampires, and many rock stars (Mick Jagger and David Bowie have certainly been around a *long time*, haven't they?) have achieved remarkable success in this field. As they say, rock & roll will never die, which makes this the perfect career choice for the Undead! While on the surface it would appear that Frank Sinatra, who has been turning up nightly in dress clothes for an eternity and who has been more than casually linked to "underworld" connections, is a vampire, I have it on good authority that Ol' Blue Eyes is *not*! A dietitian colleague of mine who specializes in vampire nutrition did an analysis of the pasta sauce Sinatra has offered for sale in supermarkets. His report: "It has enough garlic in it to put away half of Transylvania!" Enough said.

As with any musician, actors (even those in the daytime soaps), concert pianists, and late-night talk-show hosts should all be assumed to be vampires unless proven otherwise.

Whether they're celebrities or not, *all* vampires are attracted to the roar of the greasepaint, the smell of the crowd. Those who lack the talent and ego it takes to get up on a stage will cheerfully work behind the scenes as sound technicians and set designers. They know those guys get their share of groupies too. Two show biz jobs you'll *never* find a vamp working at, though, are understudy and go-fer. Vampires know that the experience they bring to whatever world they enter is incalculable, and they won't take a back seat *to* or an order *from* anybody.

Because of their exquisite taste in clothes, vampires often become haute couture fashion designers. Think about it—have you ever seen Yves St. Laurent, Valentino, or Karl Lagerfeld on a sunny day—even when they're introducing a cruisewear line? And why is it that all those runway models are so thin, and so pale?

Vampires who enjoy travel choose to become airline pilots or flight attendants. It was they who first introduced the "red-eye" shuttle, and you'll be sure to find a vampire behind the gears or in the aisles of those odd take-off times—the 9:26, 1:13, 11:44, etc.

I've never personally been involved with a fly-boy vampire, but my friend Suzanne, who has known several, tells me that, as subnormal relationships go, they can unfortunately be pretty unfulfilling. She explains, "Raspo [I guess that's short for Rasputin] will come in from Marrakech at 3:32 A.M. and leave for Kuala Lumpur at 6:28 A.M., so it will be night when he arrives, and who knows how many nights I'll be sitting up wondering when he's going to fly into my arms again?! But just when I've given up hope, he'll appear, flapping his wings [she still buys that bat myth] against my balcony door, and I'm always only too willing to put my neck on the line one more time." Suzanne mentions that, besides Raspo's own vampire attributes, his particular job does have its rewards. "You get some lovely things from Duty Free."

Government agencies such as the CIA, IRS, and FBI have recently been making major efforts to lure vampires into taking key positions in their organizations. This is part of the nation's budget-cutting measures. By hiring vampires, we will be able to eliminate the purchase of sophisticated computerized systems and high-tech information stations. Vampires don't *need* that type of technology. They *know* who the tax dodgers and serial killers are. Listen, if you'd lived for centuries, *you'd* be a great judge of character too!

The diplomatic corps is also hiring vampires to represent our country in delicate international issues. Look what happened when an ordinary (i.e., human) guy like Oliver North was given something "sensitive" to handle. We wound up with egg on our face! Oh, at first many observers thought Ollie was a vampire. Secretary Fawn Hall was a typical vampire steno, and shredding has long been known to be one of the vampire's favorite pastimes. But North didn't show the real Dracula style that a true son of shadow (Henry Kissinger definitely comes to mind) would have done in finagling himself out of a tight situation. Once he got out of that snazzy uniform and into street clothes, Ollie revealed his true self—just another dweeb who would *kill* to be a vampire.

20

You'll often find vampires at the head of high-risk, high-gain occupations like stock brokerage and money management. It's been said that the practice of insider trading was, in fact, invented by the famous Rothschild family of vampires.

There is very good reason for vampires to use any devious method they can to accumulate money. They need enough to live on—forever. They also rationalize that if they get caught trying to bilk the public, what's a few years in the slammer? They can take a long catnap or work on their memoirs. (Hey, do you think that Michael Milken . . . nah.)

Laid-back vampires will find night work as bartenders and headwaiters, but only in establishments that reek of class. They were born (well, kind of) to wear formal clothes at night, and their unctuous pandering is what gets them the big tips in the pretentious, overpriced eateries and tappies they're so at home in.

Anywhere there's a gambling casino, you'll find vampires, playing *or* dealing. Their devil-may-care attitude leads to high stakes and higher living in neon jungles like Las Vegas. Besides, in Vegas it's *normal* to go for weeks without seeing the light of day. Shrewd casino hoteliers know to keep chilled bottles of Cuvee Transylvania (a delicious, sparkling "wine" reminiscent, according to one vampire ex, of Dom Perignon but twice as costly) stocked in the minibars of the suites of high-rolling vamps.

In the mid-1980s, when it appeared everything Donald Trump (*not* a vampire—he has dandruff) touched turned to gold, it was rumored that he was planning to open several casinos just for the busy vampire market. DracWorld, Vlad's Palace, and the Black Nugget, which were all to be designed and decorated as a dark prince's dream of the netherworld, were in the works and would have attracted busloads of vampires who like to "live" on the come. It's too bad The Donald ran out of time and money before he could bring these ambitious plans to fruition. There is some speculation that Ted Turner (who has proven himself a vampire many times over by trying to mesmerize the world with "CNN News") can pick up the blueprints and make these pleasure domes a reality. It would be nice to have those roulette wheels rolling again (and in case you didn't know, black and red *is* the vampire's favorite color scheme).

Vampires make excellent dance instructors and, as cha-cha pushers, they don't even have to make an effort *not* to look like what they are. I'm going to have to break it to you, though—if you're not a well-off widow or haven't come into a hefty legacy so that you can sign up for the several lifetimes of dance lessons they're going to stick you for, your chances of getting a date with a vampire mambo maven are about nil.

It should come as no surprise that the world's greatest salesmen are vampires. With a smarmy charm, they're able to walk the fine line between seduction and domination. Whether they're pitching Rolls-Royces or romance, these characters can have you *begging* to buy into something you never wanted, don't need, can't handle, certainly can't afford, and would have been far better off without.

So you see, the vampire of your dreams can be

found hard at work in almost any profession. He can be a hair stylist (for whom women willingly submit to the most arcane tortures) a coal miner (who do you think thought up the idea of letting the canary go down first?), an advertising copywriter (could anyone but a vampire think up the well-known Manhattan slogan, "It's open all night"?), or a hotel manager (vampire necessity was the mother of the invention of room service). In fact, there's really only one job you can be sure a vampire will never take—that of a goalie on an ice-hockey team. The uniforms do nothing for him, the lights are way too bright, and the game is murder on the fangs.

❧ 3 ❧
BREAKING THE ICE
WITH A VAMPIRE

 Some years back I taught a course called "How to Flirt." Beyond eye-batting and making pointless niceties like "What a nice tie you're wearing," I advised women to develop a working knowledge of what men liked to talk about. I told them, "Be able to make conversation about sports, cars, and the latest CDs. *Then* you can bat your eyes and make pointless niceties." That course, however, was geared to flirting with *human* men. None of those sage words of wisdom will work with a vampire. When you've been around as long as he has, the outcome of one Super Bowl, the performance of one radial tire over another, and the artistic merit of the latest Tom Petty release aren't going to make a lot of impact.

More than any peppy conversation she may have practiced, the *aura* a woman gives out is what vampire guys respond to. For that matter, anything ''peppy'' will be a turn-off, and twittering banal clichés like ''have a nice day'' will have a vampire withering before your eyes. He probably hasn't had a nice *day* since the Crimean War.

Giving off a vampish aura isn't all that difficult once you throw out the criteria you've been using for what *you* think attracts these beasts to a woman. (What do *you* know, you're not a vampire!)

Body language is the essential communication between a vampire and his new conquest (that's you again). Give out long, languid, sullen, and sultry looks—the kind that would make an ordinary guy wonder if you're severely myopic or a serial killer. These are the sort of signals that let a vampire know he's caught *your* eye. When walking (prowling, really), try to mimic a model's runway gait by slithering toward him, hips thrust forward as you pivot sideways. Think this won't work? How do you think Jerry Hall, Christie Brinkley, Cindy Crawford, Paulina, and Iman got to *marry* vampires?!

Physical fitness fanatics have a lot to learn if they think competing in the Boston Marathon, pressing benches, and pumping iron will get a vampire to sit up and take notice. This doesn't mean you should burn your health club membership or trash your running shoes. Just don't go flexing your deltoids when he's around. A vampire prefers his women to be physically ''delicate.'' Words like *frail, fragile, enervated, bone-*

weary, feverish, sapped of all energy, and *drained* also come to mind. Is it any wonder so many vamps choose to become doctors!

I once used the "feather-headed" ploy to break the ice one night with a lovely stockbroker I suspected was a vampire. He had invited me to his apartment for a drink while we discussed my portfolio. After a few martinis (vampires cling to traditional cocktails—no white zinfandel spritzers for them!) I stood up, and, tottering on the new, hot pink spike-heeled pumps I'd invested in that afternoon (they *love* high heels. See Chapter 5), I giggled nervously, "Oh, the blood is *rushing* to my head! I feel a wee bit faint. . . ." Well my dears, from the look of ecstasy that crossed his face I may as well have told him I'd just hocked my rosary beads! With the velvet grace that's sum and substance of a vampire come-on, he scooped me off my size 8½s and whisked me to the dungeon, murmuring sweet words of concerned delight. It was the beginning of a brief but most broadening relationship for both me and my portfolio.

Now, some women I know would have come right out with the old, "Agghh, I feel an awful attack of PMS coming on." And that approach wouldn't have been wrong. Vampires go head over heels over those wild mood swings. But I maintain this position:

WHEN IN DOUBT ABOUT WHETHER HE'S A VAMPIRE OR NOT, BE ON THE SAFE SIDE AND FAINT.

In fact, women have used the fainting ploy to attract vampires since the play *Dracula* opened in London in 1927. A review in the *Daily Mirror* reported that the show "is full of gruesome thrills, that in the provinces, women have been carried fainting from the auditorium." *Plus ça change*, if you know what I mean.

The immutable rule of thumb for letting a vampire know you're available and interested is to behave in the most blatant, most theatrical, and most personally reprehensible way possible. Be wicked, but maintain that tinge of innocence too. The idea is to let him know that you have not yet been defiled by the ravages of blood lust, *but would certainly be open to the idea*, if the right ravager (that's him) came along.

This isn't always a cinch because it's often hard to psyche out exactly what sort of self-abasing behavior the vampire who's caught your fancy wants you to display. They give out so many mixed messages! What a vampire generally is looking for, however, is an intelligent, strong-minded, self-assured woman whose single, fatal flaw is that she will allow herself to be corrupted by him. Trust me, no vampire wants an easy lay. Mentally *or* physically.

Once you've established your willingness to be exposed to his dark side, you can move toward such subtler aspects of romance as the Silent Plea and the Whispered Regret. You don't think he's looking for the life of the party, do you? Vampires have a natural affinity for women who are slightly off balance, vaguely melancholy, thoroughly dissatisfied, and extremely confused. These are the conditions most women will try to hide from normal guys, but with the underground kings, it's perfectly all right to let it all hang out. A vampire admires a woman who will allow herself to wallow in self-doubt. Where an unenlightened regular guy might try to convince you that "You're terrific. Now snap out of that funk and get on with your life," a vampire wouldn't dream of it! The last thing he'll encourage you to do is get on with *life*.

For instance, I have a friend who has had a 10-year affair with a mega-rich, mega-married vampire. He lavishes her with all sorts of currency, flies her around the world in a private jet, bought her a Manhattan condo complete with priceless antiques, and gave her her own hearse and Renfield-driver. Does my friend do anything but mince about her treasures all day, watching endless reruns of *The Hunger* on the VCR, sniffing that "nothing *really* makes me happy anymore." When I tell her, "Miranda, you have the time and money to go to art school in Florence, cooking classes in Lyon, reindeer driving academies in Finland. Why the hell don't you *do* something," Miranda just gives me that Bambi look and plaintively responds, "But what is there to do?!" She has become the perfect vampire mistress. She was a pretty girl who had a brain, and now, with all the opportunities she has, the 10 years with the vampire have allowed her to believe that "there is *nothing* to do." She is his, and his completely.

Not every vampire is lucky enough to be a billionaire, but even the ones with merely a fistful of change can offer the power of poetry as legal tender. Poems are very important to vampires. More than moon/June/croon/tune couplets, poems are very often the tools conversation-shy vampires will use to let you know their feelings.

I recall one soft-spoken but devilishly attractive vamp shortly after we'd met sent me a poem written by one of his contemporaries, Andrew Marvell (1621–1678). It was called "To His Coy Mistress" and explained that "Had we but world enough, and time" he would have loved me 10 years before the flood! Spent a hundred years praising my eyes! And two hundred adoring each breast! Wow. The poem explained that there *wasn't* world enough and time and concluded, "Thus, though we cannot make our sun/Stand still, yet we will make him run."

Because I had some prior vampire experience by the time I'd met this prince, I knew what that shy guy was saying via those nougatty phrases. It was, "Look, babe, I just flew in from Transylvania and it'd be nice to get to know you but I don't have a lot of time so let's check into the nearest castle and get down to business." But the *way* it was said—so subtle! So romantic! So *vampiresque*!

Next time you're flirting with a vampire, see if you've got the nerve to use some of the tactics my friend Erika did when landing her guy at a week-long vampire film fest in Sausalito. (Vampires love going to things like this. You might think it would be risky, but, really, they blend right in with all of the human vamp wannabes who flock to these events. They also get to catch up on their favorite flicks and then engage in pseudoserious discussions with people who only *think* they understand the underworld. Vampires enjoy nothing if not a private joke!)

Before the butter had settled into her popcorn, she sighted her vampire of choice, and throughout the discussion after the evening's movie made herself completely obnoxious by challenging his theories, calling him a fool, and ultimately spitting in his eye in front of everybody. He found her behavior befuddling yet extraordinary—partly because it was *obvious* that she was on to his game, and partly because, during the intermission, she'd slipped him a duplicate of her hotel room key with a desperate note pleading, "Be there at midnight!" How could he resist a woman who could play *his* game so well?

Their love affair lasted the entire week (a record for Erika), and she explains its success by saying, "Vampires like being kept in the dark about what a woman really feels about them. It's giving them a dose of their own mixed messages. The idea is to make them think you're interested, then rap them across the chops. Or tell them you'll be ready at 8:00 but don't turn up until 11:00. Or don't turn up at all! Believe me, they'll respect you for it."

She offers another surefire way to break the ice with a vampire. "Tell him you're going steady, you're engaged, or you're happily married. They go gaga over inaccessible women whom they feel will be even more of a challenge to seduce. Boy, they are wicked!"

Erika confided that she keeps a wedding ring tucked into her evening bag the nights she trawls the vampire bars. When one catches her eye, she slips on the plain gold band and ingeniously informs him, "My husband is out of town tonight, but it's probably all for the best. *He doesn't understand me.*" Apparently, vampires can relate to an old chestnut like that, and according to Erika, it gets you where you're going—either his crypt or yours.

At this point, I can just hear you saying to yourself, "Has this woman gone over the deep end? Why in the world would telling a vampire I'm engaged make him more interested in me?" I know, I know. It sounds all too *human*, doesn't it? But you must remember that every vampire was, at one time or another, just that—a living, breathing, human male. Becoming a vampire does many things to a man (for starters, it makes him prone to *terrible* sunburns), but one thing it does *not* do is change the nature of the beast. If anything, it heightens that nature so that your vampire is even *more* ruled by such guy factors as territoriality, testosterone, and tackling a challenge.

You don't have to take just my word for it. Go out and get a video of *Dracula*. Watch it. Who does our babe Drac go for? Is it clueless, kind of homely, *available* Lucy? Oh, sure, he shows her a good time, but before you know it she's one drained damsel who's learned the hard way that being easy doesn't guarantee you'll be respected, adored, or even *around* the next morning. No, no, no. The one who gets all the goodies—the true love, the romance, the passionate angst, the great sex—is *the one who's supposed to be getting married real soon.* She's the one he sets his cap (or rather, his cape) for. Just like real life, no?

If, however, you're too shy to take Erika's dynamic approach to vampiring, perhaps you can get to know him better by showing an interest in his hobbies. If your new vamp has an art collection, for example, let him show it off to you. Be sure to make insightful comments like, "What interesting Romanian art you have—and so much of it!" Agree with him that surrealism is downright tacky. Have a laugh on Dalí and applaud his taste in realists like weird-art-guy Hieronymus Bosch, whose tortured visions "tell it like it is."

Vampires are also crack gamesmen. They shine at Go, an ancient (could it be anything else?) game of strategy in which two players compete to acquire territory. "Life and death" and "to escape or not to escape" are part of the learning process in this elegant and unsettling game. Vampires also like to play chess—backing an opponent into a corner is a move they excel in. It's been rumored that a vampire invented Charades, Pictionary, and Trivial Pursuit, all of which embrace his abiding faith that style is more important—or at least more entertaining—than substance.

Vampires, of course, generally excel in languages, so you may want to break the ice by using a few catchy bon mots like "*de mortuis nil nisi bonum*" (Latin for "Say nothing but good of the dead") or "*Du bist was Du isst*" (German for "You are what you eat"). Or try something a bit more *moderne* like "*Avez-vous la nostalgie de la boue,*" which is French for "Do you have a yearning for the low life?"

Ultimately, to break the ice with a vampire, you must learn the fine art of lying. Lie about your age, your weight, where you're from, where you're going, what you think, what you've done, and what you want. The lie, after all, is the vampire's language of love.

৯৮ 4 ৯৯
YOUR FIRST DATE

 You'll always remember your first date with a vampire. This can mean it will have been either a very good or a very bad experience, but you can rest assured that he'll do his darnedest to make the occasion a once-in-a-lifetime event (I'll leave it up to you to figure out *whose* lifetime we're talking about. . . .)

Although it is unlikely your vampire will ask you to make suggestions about what to do on your first date (this isn't *just* a control thing; he also has had quite a bit of experience in orchestrating these magic moments), should he be magnanimous enough to ask, "Is there anything in particular *you'd* like to do," refrain at all costs from replying, "Oh, I have some interesting

friends you'd just love to get to know. Let's go double."
That type of suggestion is an unforgivable breach of
vampire dating etiquette. First off, he'd met everyone
he'd "love to get to know" by 1843. Second, a vampire
has a limited attention and energy span, and you don't
want to get off on the wrong foot exhausting *him.*
Third, he's going to hate your friends as a matter of
principle. The simple "You make the decisions for
both of us, darling" will ensure you a much more
carefree night.

You'll need to learn to expect the unexpected when
dating a vampire, and it won't be long until you're put
to the test.

Because of his delicate nature and erratic schedule, a vampire can't always be where he says he will be.
Even if he promised faithfully to pick you up at 7:18
sharp! While you're waiting for him to call and explain
his absence, use your time wisely. Finally get around to
reading Marcel Proust's *Remembrance of Things Past*—
all three volumes. Then learn French and reread it in
the original. Take up a correspondence course in voo-
doo or tarot reading—or both. You never know when
you're going to need skills like these. Complete the
life-size needlepoint of Rembrandt's "The Night
Watch" that's been sitting in the back of your closet
since that vacation in Amsterdam. Curry favor with an
older relative who may look upon you as trust fund
material. (If you get serious with your vampire, you're
going to need the occasional windfall.) Begin a garden
of exotic night-blooming plants like deadly nightshade.
Do *something* that will eat up a great deal of your
precious waiting time.

Once your vampire *does* appear to collect you (and he will, you're not going to get off that easily), you'll be whirled into an exciting stratosphere where he'll make you Queen of the Night.

Here are some rules of vampire etiquette you'll need to know so you don't make a gaffe on the first date.

VAMPIRE ETIQUETTE

♥ *1. If you're at a cocktail bar or a restaurant, tell* him, *not the server, that you'd like a Missionary's Downfall (a well-known vampire libation) and the rack of lamb.* He prefers to order for *madame* and may misconstrue your eye contact and conversation with the server (particularly if the server is attractive) as a flirtation. To a vampire, the slightest flirtation with another man is tantamount to betrayal. It's too early in the game to let you in on what betrayal is tantamount to.

♥ *2. Even if you're a Cordon Bleu graduate, let* him *order the wine.* He takes pride in his knowledge of oenology. While at first gulping a strong, sweet Cotnari (Romania's most famous wine) may seem

a little rough with the Dover sole you ordered, think of it as his way of introducing you into his world. Any fool who's
picked up a How to Impress a Date man-
ual would have ordered Chardonnay.

▼ *3. Bring plenty of cash and credit cards
with you.* You may not have to use them
but, as previously mentioned, his schedule
(not to mention his intentions!) may be
sketchy, and having funds to make a quick
getaway is a definite advantage. I can say
this from personal experience. Every vampire I've ever been out with—from brain
surgeons to mail clerks—have had either
a beeper or a portable phone they tote
around with them. This allows them to
take important messages from Renfield
that defy explanation but result in your
vampire flying out of the restaurant and
into the night on a moment's notice.

Like the first date I had with a vampire attorney
(night court, natch). He took me to a bizarre Moroc-
can restaurant where belly dancers performed wantonly
and we were seated on plush velvet cushions in a private
alcove. *Tres romantique, non?* Midway between sips of
raki and fingersful of couscous, his beeper rang. He
dashed out to make a call, and returned highly agi-
tated.

"What's the matter?" I asked.

"I can't tell you. I don't want you to worry," he replied.

"I hardly know you. What could be happening in your life that would worry me?" I reasoned.

"Trust me," he said, brushing my lips before promising to return. He disappeared into the moon night.

Around 2:00 A.M., as the last belly dancer jingle-jangled her way out of the dive, I figured he wasn't coming back. So I paid the check and taxied home.

The following month, he called as if nothing untoward had occurred and asked if we could get together "for another great night on the town." By then, I'd met a vampire who lived in my building and would be easier to keep track of, so I declined the invite. You know the old saying, "So many vampires, so little time!"

Unless you live close to some scenic wonder such as Carlsbad Caverns or another trendy "underground" locale where a vampire may feel comfortable during the day, your first date will decidedly be in the P.M.—often very late in the P.M. A midnight movie, a quick bite at some tucked-away restaurant where gypsy violins play, a late-night mass at some gothic cathedral, a romantic moonlit stroll through Forest Lawn—all are strong possibilities for your first evening with a vampire.

One vampire I used to go out with (an adorable artist type who looked amazingly like a young Jack Nicholson—Jack never even *tried* to hide it, did he!) insisted that our first "night on the town" begin at 10:06 P.M. At first I thought he was just another cheapskate trying to get out of buying me dinner. Later I learned his true motive. Ours was a summer love, you see, and daylight saving time made it impossible for him to fly into my arms any sooner.

That particular vampire's idea of a fun first date was to take me (would you believe it!) camping. Since my idea of roughing it amounts to staying in a hotel that doesn't have 24-hour room service, I was less than intrigued—*until* he told me we'd be roughing it just a few blocks from my home, which was in Philadelphia's historical district. The site he'd settled on was St. Peter's Cemetery.

Around 3:00 A.M. on an August night, as we clambered over the iron portals, a police car stopped and the officer (who had every right) leaned out the window and asked us just what the hell we were doing. Like all vampires, especially Irish vampires, my date had a gift of the improvised gab. As he gave me the last hoist over the gate, he yelled back to the cop, "We're a writer/photographer team. We're doing a fashion layout." Sure enough, the cop bought it and left us alone with the dead.

The gravestones at St. Peter's go back centuries (looking at all those ancient markers sort of made me wonder whether this first date was going to turn into a *family affair*, if you know what I mean). After careful deliberation, we chose a sturdy 1857 slab on which to have a lie-down. The air was thick and still and I could taste the earth, even through my nose. We talked in whispers, wondering who it was we'd kicked out of bed. I must have dozed off at one point, and it was very peaceful wafting in and out of dreams and the moistly tepid predawn fog that was wafting over the city. Maybe all that fresh air made me a bit drowsy. Then again, maybe it was the old MF (Mesmerization Factor) at work—all I know is that the minute he covered me with his cape (to protect me from the cold, he said. *Uh huh*, I thought, before my brain went on standby), things got a tad fuzzy, in a heady sort of way. I also remember feeling something lightly scraping my throat—just lightly, mind you, but enough to make me wonder whether Renfield had forgotten to take out the tag when the cloak came back from the cleaners. It's *so hard* to find good help these days. . . .

I *do* know I wasn't scared. Sometimes when you're doing crazy, dumb, nonsensical things with a vampire (as I was that night), you tend to make yourself watch instead of admitting you're part of the action. It's as if you're seeing what's happening through a camera, which makes it easier to tell yourself, "Gee, I'm in a vampire movie!" Perhaps deluding yourself that "it's just a movie" is what allows you to believe you're safe.

Anyway, we climbed out of the cemetery at about 5:43 and kissed goodnight; he went his way, I went mine. I can't say the date was as much fun as dining and dancing at the Rainbow Room, but I'm glad I didn't decline the opportunity to see how the other half "lives." And I'm happy to report that, considering how reckless I was that night (after all, I hardly *knew* him!), I managed to survive the date with nary a scratch—although for the next week or so I sported a rather large hickey on my neck (boy, those dry cleaner tags really pack a wallop!).

Speaking of the Rainbow Room, don't expect to

be going anyplace too posh on your first vampire date. These guys, no matter how many rubles, lire, francs, and greenbacks they've managed to squirrel away through the centuries, tend to downplay the whole dining experience. For sure you won't be going to any Italian or French bistros that reek of garlic. But you already know that.

If he does want to wine and dine you, he'll take you to a romantic, dimly lit Hungarian restaurant where all the servers look like Bela Lugosi—or at least dress like him—and plaintive gypsy music fills the air. I don't pretend to know much about gypsy music, but a vampire I once met in Brussels (gorgeous, Hungarian, silver-haired, *and* Undead under the murky sign of Cancer) explained the basics to me. He had taken me to a sweet little Magyar eatery not far from the city's glittery Grande Palace. (Brussels, by the way, is teeming with handsome vampires.) Over tureens of icy slivovitz, we listened to a group of six violinists, all tarted up in their embroidered gypsy shirts, pantaloons, and boots. Gregor (my vampire of the night) explained that when a song gypsies play sounds melancholy, it's actually a cheerful ditty. Conversely, when a tune sounds like a real knee-slapper, the lyrics are verging on the suicidal. Having been an observer of Gregor's confounding mood swings, this made all the sense in the world to me.

Other favorite first dates for vampires are poetry-reading soirées and the ballet. If there are no live performances worth catching the night of your date, a vampire may take you to an art cinema to catch revivals of Nureyev and Baryshnikov films. (A vampire choreographer once confided to me that these Russian ballerinos were best captured on camera. He told me, "Hon, those boys never had a *live* performance. Know what I mean?")

Vampires love to dance, and several have told me how delighted they are that discos, which were so popular in the late 1970s, are making a comeback. They enjoy taking a date to a joint where the music pulsates, strobe lights create confusing, swirling patterns, and all-important body language counts more than stilted small talk. If on your first date a vampire takes you to a crowded, underground disco where the bartenders hasten to mix his "regular," and the stunning cloakroom attendant with the luminescent skin and the Band-Aid on her neck glares at you with loathing in her eyes, you'll know he thinks you're special enough to show you off to all of his pals. And make no mistake—that's exactly what's happening.

Most vampires maintain memberships in many afterhours clubs. These clubs can be elegant penthouses where soft jazz, a magnificent view of the city *à nuit*, and vintage champagne corks popping is part of the ambience. Or they can be beer-soaked tenements where you're lucky if you can find a stale pretzel and a ladies room. Regardless, he will drag you to his haunts because vampires only want to call it a night when *le bon Dieu* decides to call it a night by making the sun rise again. Pop a few Nō-Dōz and be proud he's taking you along to have "one for the road." It means your first date was a rousing success!

▼ ▼ ▼

Of course, the question that's bound to come up on your first date with a vampire is, "How far do you go?"

I certainly can't answer that for any woman. Just how far you stick your neck out is a sensitive, individual issue. Do what you feel in your heart is right, but use your brain as well. Which brings up the subject of safe sex. Now, we know the reason it's important to use protection with ordinary men is that we don't know whom they've been with. Like everything else, it's just the opposite with vampires. The reason to practice safe sex with them is because we know they've been with just about *everybody*.

❧ 5 ❧
DRESSING FOR YOUR VAMPIRE

Once you've caught a vampire's eye, one of the surest ways you can keep his interest is via a provocative wardrobe. Remember, this vampire guy has royal blood (along with every other kind) coursing through his veins, and he'll want the woman he's chosen to look every inch a princess. And you know that old Transylvanian saying, "If you look like a princess, if you act like a princess, if you *dress* like a princess, well, you must be a princess!"

The two things vampires can't bear their women to be are commonplace and casual. If you show up for a date dressed in your dreary dress-for-success business suit or your straight-from-the-gym grungy sweats, you won't be a vampire's date for long. "Life is too short to be ordinary,'' a wise old couturier vampire once told me.

Before you say, ''Hey, the way I dress reflects my personality and comfort is important to me and I'm not going to let some vampire walk into my life and then turn myself inside out just to please him,'' let me suggest that many women who've held that intelligent view have, in time, found it an enormous kick to wear some of the items they would never have dreamed of purchasing had they not met a man of midnight. Like shamelessly sexy lingerie.

And underwear is where it all starts. Keep in mind what a famous historian vampire once pronounced in his memoirs: ''The most devastating catastrophe to occur in the last four centuries was the invention of pantyhose.'' Vampires hate pantyhose almost as much as they hate to see a cross coming their way. Vampires are romantic. Pantyhose are not. I'll rephrase that. Vampires are sexy. Pantyhose are not.

So, start out by investing in a few frilly garter belts and silky stockings. And forget about doing the all-black number. Most vampires I've known like to see women in pale shades of scanties—like a slender, creamy, lace and satin garter belt holding up the palest peach stockings.

Flower-petal-soft corselets studded with tiny satin rosebuds and bows, lacy camisoles, flirty crinolines (over the aforementioned garter belt, stockings, and ruffled panties) are guaranteed to excite him. Actually, they'll get *most* guys hot under the collar but the vampire guy in particular. They blend the sweet memories of his erotic past (when all women dressed that way) with the very real *now*.

Once you've put yourself together and look a little like a centerfold in a Victoria's Secret catalog, how do you let him *know* what little treasures you have in store for him? Not wearing anything over your bustier and girdle à la Madonna is definitely ixnay. I say this because every vampire guy I've ever met has found the Material Girl's brazen, bare-it-all style thoroughly unappealing. *I* think she's pretty cool, but so many vampires have said she was "scary," I wonder if the Undead have a sharper perception of her than I do.

Here's how to finesse your way into letting your vamp guy know what's lurking under your "innocent" sweater and skirt or cocktail frock. You can begin with the old, "Oh, I just dropped my (fill in: lap-top computer, membership card to the Druid Society, autographed copy of *Queen of the Damned*)." Then, ever so gracefully, bend over to retrieve it so that he is able to get a gander of lace, cleavage, and whatever else is available.

One woman I know used an even more coquettish ploy. She had been out on a late dinner date with a vamp and was fetchingly outfitted in a can't-lose, low-cut black silk sheath and black five-inch-heeled pumps. In the back seat of a taxi on their way back to his place, she lounged in a corner of the cab, flung herself over his knees, and revealed a great deal of what the evening held in store. Alas, not only was her vampire bedazzled, the fellow driving in the next lane, who got a great view of the garter belt hiding beneath that dress, was distracted as well. What she displayed created a minor collision. No one was hurt, thank heavens, but by the time the taxi driver and the offending motorist had finished exchanging blows and insurance carriers, the magic of the moment was gone for good. The slight hike of a skirt, the quick peek of a boned, half-cup bra under a low-cut silk shirt, the belt that encircles a waspish waist are less dangerous methods of letting him know what's behind the scenes.

As for outerwear, don't feel that vampires only go for the basic black "Morticia" gown (although you should have one of these go-everywhere numbers in your closet). Following are a variety of outfits that always make the Vampire Best-Dressed List.

- ♥ A white, low-necked poet shirt with long, full sleeves tucked into tight pants that are tucked into stiletto-heeled boots.
- ♥ A smartly tailored suit (with a very short skirt), high heels, silk V-neck blouse, pearls, and a hat with a veil (think early Faye Dunaway).
- ♥ A black, backless cocktail sheath (can be long or short, but make sure it exposes plenty of jugular).
- ♥ A regal velvet dressing gown worn over a white, low-necked ruffled nightdress.

- ♥ *Red!* Red high heels, red lips, red hips, red hair, red satin ribbons everywhere. Red, Red, Red!
- ♥ For more demure moments . . . *pink!* Pink angora sweaters, pink ballerina slippers, pink lips, pink slips, and every other possible place for PINK!

Flowing capes with hoods, rustling petticoats, embroidered petticoats—these are the clothes a vampire likes to see a woman in—and out of. If you need to get more of a fix on what to wear, rent *Gone with the Wind, The French Lieutenant's Woman, Henry and June,* or any other movie that depicts the century your vamparamour may be nostalgic about.

Once you've got your wardrobe under control, be prepared to model it *for his eyes only.* Here's what I mean.

It's summer. You've got on the tiny white lace top, tight white shorts, and high-heeled sandals vampires like to look at in July. You and your vampire are on the widow's walk watching the fireflies come out and get eaten by the mosquitoes. You decide you want to go to the corner store to get ice cream/buy a racing form/call an exorcist. This is the conversation that will ensue:

HIM: You're going out dressed like *that!?*
YOU: Why not? What's wrong?

47

HIM: You shouldn't go out alone dressed like
    that.
YOU: Why?
HIM: You know very well why.

Maybe you *don't* know why, but he certainly does. He knows you will attract other guys with intentions as base as his. Which is all well and good when he's there to monitor their—and your—actions. It's not OK, however, when you're going out on your own. So, if you're really intent on going to the corner store, he'll probably convince you to change into a chador. If you refuse, he'll find some lame excuse to tag along. The third option is that he'll find a way to change your mind about leaving the castle.

Before you get the vaulted notion that he must be so obsessed with you he fears you'll be swept away by another, kindly face, a little reality. A vampire is not jealous so much as he is possessive. Jealousy requires more singlemindedness than any vampire is capable of.

What you do with your hair also falls into the category of vampire dressing. It's well known that vampires like women with long hair that's pulled back off the neck or regally piled high on the head (not only is it a romantic look, but it also gives your vamp an unobstructed view of your throat). Some vampires, though, prefer boyish coifs.

Mr. Ivan, a noted Hollywood vampire stylist, re-lates, "The idea of vampires wanting their women to have long, dark hair parted in the middle and flowing over their shoulders is as narrow-minded as saying we're only turned on by AB-type blood! Who do you think invented the Beehive? The Shag? The Page Boy? The Ivana Slut-Puppy Look? Vampires, that's who!"

Mr. Ivan continues, "On the one hand, it's very sexy to 'disrobe' a woman by pulling her hair from her neck either strand by strand or in one vicious grasp. On the other hand, a woman with very short hair can look so vulnerable . . . so sweet . . . you just want to eat her up." According to Mr. Ivan, vampires also admire spiky, punk hairdos as well as Crayola-colored green, purple, yellow-orange, and jet-black crowning glories. Mr. Ivan's advice is, "Don't be afraid to perm, spray, color, distort, shave it off, or let it grow to the ground. Vampires admire the extreme in all things. Your worst mistake would be to show up looking like a suburban matron on her way to the big sale at the local mall. You know how we hate the ordinary!"

Your vampire won't disappoint you when it comes to *his* duds. Clothes mean a lot to a vampire. They are a form of identification, much like a driver's license or social security card is to an ordinary guy. In some cases, they are the only form of identification he has!

Some vampires like to dress upper-crust Savile Row. Others go Armani. You'll find biker vampires all in leather, surfer-boy vampires, vampires duded up as cowboys or as foreign legionnaires. For some reason, uniforms strike their fancy, so don't be surprised when you find the cute cop on the beat, the sexy postman, or our nation's armed forces generals are vampires in disguise.

A Clothing Conundrum—To Turtleneck or Not to Turtleneck?

Since biblical times, vampires have known that a woman's J-spot (the jugular) is her most sensitive zone of physical arousal. However, engaging in J-spot activities with a vampire will often leave your neck sporting embarrassing red marks commonly known as puncture wounds, but which I prefer to call hickeys.

If you're the shy type and want to hide your love-bites, a turtleneck shirt or sweater, a prettily tied ascot or scarf, or a massive choker will do the trick. Some women opt for cover-all cosmetics. I personally cannot vouch for those melt-away products.

The question you must confront is, "Do I want to hide these symbols of passion or do I want to let the world know I'm a vampire girl?"

Then ask yourself, "What would *he* want me to do?"

If the answers you receive propel you into packing up all your high-necked clothes and shipping them off to Goodwill, you know you're more than a little in love with a vampire.

✣ 6 ✣
INTRODUCING
HIM TO YOUR PARENTS

Bringing a vampire home to meet the folks is a little like turning up with an out-of-work juggler or a vacationing terrorist. You know you're going to have to make up plenty of excuses and invent the rest.

Before you even *think* of exposing him to your parents, you must reassure your vamp that Mom and Dad aren't out to drive a stake through his heart or spray bat pesticide at him. His apprehension is understandable, considering the ordeals he's been put through by parents through the centuries.

You might also begin assuaging his fears by letting it slip that your family is "dysfunctional." This will immediately make him feel at home because vam-

pires, as we all know, came from the original dysfunctional family.

Brag a little about having been brought up with a
control-crazed dad, an all-too-fragile mom, slightly
batty siblings, and an uncle who takes all his meals in
a closet.

Once he thinks he'll fit in, it's just a question of
setting up the intros. It is most unlikely that the first
meeting will go well, but with careful planning, you
can avoid some of the uglier confrontations that might
occur.

Let's start by taking the worst case scenario. It's
winter, so the sun should be down by 6:00 P.M. You've
invited your new vampire to meet your folks over a
Sunday supper.

After the obligatory uncomfortable introductions,
Dad asks him to sit down in front of the TV where a
ball game of absolutely no consequence to your vamp is
making zigzag patterns on the screen.

Dad asks him what he'd like to drink, and here's
where it starts to unravel. Your vampire won't know
this is one of Dad's dumb tests, so, instead of respond-
ing "iced tea" or "a beer like you're having, sir," he
will, with all the archness of Jeremy Irons in a smoking
jacket (which your vamparamour will probably be wearing anyway), respond, "A pousse-café would be nice.
But if it's too much trouble, a Vodka Stinger will do."

This sort of answer will make Dad very suspi-
cious. As well it should! No normal man asks for an
after-dinner drink *before* supper. So if he's not a nor-

mal guy and Dad knows you're crazy about him, he'll have it figured out in jig time that he's let a vampire into the living room.

Once Dad is sure he's got him cornered, he'll get into his Professor Van Helsing mode and start to bombard your vampire guy with the questions you've been having nightmares about, like:

"So, how many times have you been married?"

"You wouldn't happen to have a day job, would you?"

"Do you *own* that castle, or are you renting it?"

"What exactly is it that you *do*, son?"

The best way to skirt these embarrassing issues is to arrange to have this critical first meeting on neutral turf—anywhere but *home*.

Several women I know who've been through this parent/vampire ritual have informed me that it is best held late (quite late) in the afternoon at some swanky hotel where afternoon tea is served. Mom will be enchanted by the puffy little pastries and creamy doodads; Dad will think your guy's a poofter, which is somewhat better than him thinking he's a vampire.

A vampire historian has indicated in a recent book that the British invented the ludicrous practice of serving afternoon tea for the express purpose of easing the gulf between a vampire and his girlfriend's parents. Why else, the book asks, would anyone choose to have tea and tarts at 5:00 P.M. when white wine and buffalo wings are so much more appropriate—unless there is a "darker" reason?

Teatime with the folks allows a vampire to:

1. Show them how well he behaves in public places.
2. Prove he doesn't *have* to have a drink just because the sun is down.
3. Get off the hook in less than an hour. Teatime waitresses like to shuffle the Darjeeling and Earl Grey drinkers out to make room for the "live" ones who order doubles and leave large tips.

Some friction may occur when the bill comes. You *know* your guy doesn't like to carry around cash or credit cards and wouldn't want to pay for tea and cookies as a matter of principle. Yet if Dad is forced to pick up the tab, he'll always be able to say, "I knew he was a deadbeat from the very first time he stiffed us at tea!"

Here's how to handle this dicey contretemps: prepay! That's right. Give the hostess your credit card before being seated. Tell her the bill for your party is to be put on it with a handsome 20 percent tip, sign it, and *voilà*! When the last dollop of Devonshire cream is carted away and Dad's waiting to see your guy look like a scuzzball, you can calmly say, "Oh, Vlad (or whatever your vamp's name is) has taken care of it already." That'll show the old geezer!

This floating credit card ploy can meet with some disastrous results if Vlad has been seeing the hostess on the side, but what is love without trust, I always say.

Even if the afternoon tea ceremony worked like a charm, Dad still won't be all that keen on your vampire. But Mom will. I've seen many a Mom all atwitter after they've met their daughters' new vamps. They make insipid comparisons like, "Oh, he reminds me so much of Richard Chamberlain in (fill in the miniseries)." The fact your vampire looks more like Richard III than Richard Chamberlain will have no impact on *madame mère*. That's because vampires know how to handle women, and since Mom is a woman, he'll have so mesmerized her that, after the tea is over, she'll think *she* was his date!

He may even stop by Mom's some evening when you're working late and Dad's off at his bowling league "just to say hello." She'll be pleased when he shows interest in the personal effects she takes pride in—be it her collection of British biscuit tins or her long, manicured fingernails that remind him of the great times he spent with the mandarins of ancient China.

He will have been thoughtful enough to arrive with a small gift—like a box of licorice. Licorice is one of the Undead's preferred flavors, and they seem to think that real people like it as well. He might even suggest that Mother join the two of you at one of those Hungarian bistros some night. She will be delighted. You will start becoming as leery as Pop.

Until you're ready to introduce your vampire to your mother vis-à-vis, don't talk about him to her over the phone. From your halting responses, the catch in your throat, and your uncontrollable sobs, she will be able to pick up that you are involved with an *awful* man who is making your life a misery. Once she meets him, however, she will applaud your choice and direct all her attention his way, blithely ignoring that you've lost a considerable amount of weight, have developed a slight tremor in your upper lip, and have ghastly dark shadows under your eyes.

With all her good intentions, Mom may cause a spark of trouble between you and your new vamp. She'll want to know more about his family—no, not the wife and kids—his *forebears*. She'll ask questions about his ancestry, where his "people" are from, what business they're engaged in, and why they don't seem to exist.

Since you can't very well tell her he's descended from a line of bloodthirsty princes who've been around for hundreds of years, it might be the greater part of valor to go to the "they all died in an avalanche skiing in Gstaad one mournful winter day" route. Not only will this get her sympathy, she'll be impressed. All Moms know that celebrities like Elizabeth Taylor Fortensky, Roger Moore, and Julie Andrews spend their winter holidays at that swell Swiss ski resort.

As far as handling Dad goes, there are ways to neutralize a father, depending on your Vlad's arrogance level. Here's how my friend Marie's vampire did it.

Marie had been on vacation on the isle of Capri. There she met Pierluigi, an Italian vampire who combined the physical beauty of the Renaissance with a contemporary approach ("darling, you handle everything so much better than me. Why don't *you* do it?")

to women. Like most vampires, he liked to travel and accumulate green cards, so he followed Marie back to the States, where he passionately wooed her.

She was mad about him, even though it was difficult to keep up with his torrid nights of love while working two jobs, cooking his meals, and washing his clothes while he lay around all day writing a script for a film about lesbian-nun drug dealers he hoped would be produced by Francis Ford Coppola.

What with Pierluigi's sketchy past and nonexistent present, Marie was terrified about how her parents would react to him. Yet she knew she couldn't put off a meeting forever. What she hadn't counted on was Pierluigi's brazen fecklessness.

When he entered her parents' living room, he looked her father Undead in the eye and with that yummy accent declared, "Signore, I love your daughter and I want her to marry me."

That took the old man back a few paces. It took Marie back as well, since Pierluigi had never mentioned tying the knot to *her*.

It was, however, a brilliant stratagem. Dads don't believe vampires ever have good intentions (they don't—Pierluigi no more wanted to marry Marie than he wanted to get a job), but Pierluigi put him off balance. For the rest of the night, Dad was sizing him up, not as a creature of the night, but as a potential son-in-law. Pierluigi was still way off the mark in what Dad had in mind for his "little pumpkin," but at least he was being treated like a two-bit gigolo—*not* a down-and-out vampire.

I'm not going to waste time dealing with your brothers' or sisters' reactions to your vampire. They most likely won't even notice anything odd about him. They've got their own spooks and witches to worry about.

Hopefully, you've now got enough ammo to get you through the vampire/parents face-off. Here are just a few more words to the wise:

1. Keep all meetings short, sweet, and after sundown.
2. Beg your vampire to show up looking *somewhat* normal—no velvet capes, puh-leeze!
3. If he does show up in costume, tell your parents he's in a road company of *Phantom*.
4. Keep all stakes, garlic, and mirrors out of sight.
5. Keep the conversation *light*—don't even let it *graze* topics like politics, religion, conservationism, the greenhouse effect, the death penalty, holes in the ozone layer, animal rights, sports, nuclear power, what he does for a living, TV sit-

coms, world hunger, *anything* that might trigger off his volatile nature. I realize this limits the chatter to Pre-Raphaelite paintings and the many wonderful flavors and shades of Brazilian coffee. But you want this to be as pleasant as possible, don't you?

❧ 7 ❧
YOUR VAMPIRE
AND OTHER WOMEN

Women are fatally attracted to vampires. You already know that. Well, maybe not *all* women, but I'm not so sure I trust or understand the ones who aren't. Like my old school chum, Nancy.

One summer night, Nancy and I were at a seashore bar that was packed with preppy vegetation. Across the room, I spotted a Nicolas Cage type off in a corner, moodily nursing the vodka rocks cupped in his long, Rachmaninoff hands. His eyes were slightly slanted, giving him an exotic Eurasian look. Either that or it wasn't his first vodka rocks. A shock of dark hair veiled his caterpillar eyebrows. Although it was a scorcher of a summer night, he wore a black leather jacket and hadn't a trace of tan.

"Isn't he *gorgeous*," I screeched to Nancy, pointing out the obvious vampire in the crowd.

"He's a creep," she responded.

Thinking she might have thought I was referring to the hail-fellow-well-met halfback trying to get his section of the bar to join him in the Notre Dame fight song, I redirected her attention to My Guy.

"I knew who you meant," she snippily retorted. "The guy who looks like he just checked out of the Bates Motel."

Nancy made me feel like a fool. Oh, not about my impeccably contaminated taste in *men*, but in my misreading of *other women*!

Women like Nancy—sensible, down-to-earth women who never cut classes to see a Gerard Depardieu movie; who never woke up at 4:00 A.M. with excruciating leg cramps from dancing the night away in five-inch-heeled red satin sandals; who honestly believe that electronic massage instruments were created to help tired muscles; who never quite got the hang of *torment*—just don't fall for the lure of a vampire. What luck! It whittles the competition down to a mere couple of million!

But those couple of million are tough and determined and you have to keep a keen, vigilant eye out for them. The most benign variety is the vampire groupie who, like the rock star groupie, just wants to hang around anyone who can do her some harm. These types generally are content to make do with a Renfield, just as rock groupies have been known to keep company with the sound and lighting technicians when the star

61

of the show is unavailable. They hurt no one, with the possible exception of themselves.

The women you really have to watch out for are the ones like you and me—women who know, love, understand, and will accept no substitute for the vampire guy. Like you and me, these women are clever, devious, ruthless, and demoralizing. They'll put you off your guard by stating, "There are no good vampires around. They're all either married, gay, or in hibernation for the next century. I'm not even going to bother anymore." But bother they *do*. And the next time you're at a party or a pub with a potential vampire sweetie, sure enough, one of them will make her move by quoting Yeats, flashing more neck than absolutely necessary, and yakking away about any past or current event she can describe as "a bloodbath." She will be the friend who, at the last minute, will cancel any plans she's made with a woman buddy if she thinks she's got the slimmest chance of even having "just a bite" with a vampire. While it's comforting to carp, "her needs are so desperate, so obvious, I feel *sorry* for her," this type of woman gets more than her fair share of vampires—she's getting yours and mine! And, to add insult to injury, you know that she's right about one thing: most of the good ones *are* taken.

But the good news is that whole new generations of vampires are becoming Undead every night. The bad news, of course, is that every single last one of them will be an outrageous flirt who will make you queasy with jealousy and shaky with suspicion. And there's nothing you can do about it.

If you think you're going to be able to stop a vampire from flirting with other women, you'd better steal yourself for some rude awakenings. Vampires are *born* (or, should I say, *reborn*) to flirt. It's in their nature.

And let me tell you something else. Coping with his night-to-night flirtatiousness will still be *a day at the beach* compared to dealing with his long, complicated past that's been filled with beautiful, desirable women. Even that wouldn't be so bad, if only he didn't feel compelled to tell you all about it.

One of the major differences between vampires and ordinary men is the way they handle the other women in their lives. Most normal guys mention they've "been around the track a few times" and leave it at that. A vampire, who is generally so secretive he doesn't want to let on what time of day (rather, night) it is, practically *gushes* about his past conquests! He's driven to go into luridly gorgeous detail about the fascinating women who've crammed his amatory past. He'll give you vivid descriptions of the fabulous women he's smitten and bitten—so vivid you'll start worrying that you're in competition with legendary sirens like Jean Harlow, Mata Hari, Marilyn Monroe, or Greta Garbo. And since he *is* a vampire, you very well may be.

To make things even rougher on you, if you're a vampire girl, you'll be only too willing to hang on every word of his pompous narration.

Here's a sad but typical tale. I was on a second date with one of my vampire boyfriends (I'm not sure

if this one was Irish, but his name *was* Sean Patrick).
We had tucked into a quaint, remote bed & breakfast
outside Boston for a weekend. (Vampires adore
"quaint" and "remote.")

During dinner on Friday night, he went on at
great length about a long-term affair he'd had with a
woman named Serena. (They're never named anything
normal like Jane or Kate. It's always something like
Serena.) Like others of his ilk, he gave no time frame
to the affair like, "Serena and I went to the Live-Aid
Concert" or "Serena and I were in Berlin when the
Wall fell" or "Serena and I were at the Winter Olym-
pics in Albertville." It keeps you guessing whether it
was a World War II affair or if it had ended the night
before you went out with him.

He did make it clear, though, that he and Serena
had done some pretty wonderful things together. He
told me about the romance of being in costume for
Carnival in Venice, how beautiful she looked when they
went hot air ballooning by moonlight through the
Alps, how enormous the marlin was they caught when
they were fishing off Dakar; how sweet she was when
they were trekking through Persia (I guess it *was* a long
time ago, Persia's been Iran since 1935). . . .

Now you have to understand, he was telling me all
of this after checking *me* into a ratty $30 a night B &
B after having taken me to an equally ratty Mexican
cantina for a taco dinner! But here's the problem. I
wasn't doing anything to stop the torture of listening
to his tales of this long-ago love. Why did I let him go
on?! Why didn't I say, "Enough of this, Sean Patrick.

If Serena was so damn terrific, why aren't you with her tonight? Aside from the fact she's probably been dead for the last 200 years."

The reason I let him go on is simplicity itself. He was a vampire, and his stories about the women in his life were so compelling, so fraught with the fractured beauty of a great love lost, it was impossible for me not to listen and to project, "Someday *I'll* be the great love. . . . But this time, it will *work*."

The belief that we can be that one great love, the love that makes him no longer ease out of his tomb to take other women out on cheap dates and use the old lines that have been getting them into bed for centuries, is what keeps most of us vampire gals hooked on the stories of his thousand and one nights. And while it's a lovely daydream, there's a point where we have to face up to it being a staggering waste of time.

Vampires don't change. They can't. And, as I am sure the sun will rise tomorrow, when my old beau Sean Patrick is in yet another quaint, cheap B & B with someone just like me, he'll be reciting *la belle histoire* of his magical time with *moi*—a lousy two-night stand!

Vampire guys have the uncanny, *unnatural* ability to make the shabbiest of past encounters seem as though they were earth-shattering romances, to be put in the same love boat as Anthony and Cleopatra, Napoléon and Josephine, Charles Parnell and Kitty O'Shea, Robert Browning and Elizabeth Barrett, Ozzie and Harriet, Lucy and Desi.

If you have the strength of spirit (which I rarely

can muster, I'm afraid), you *can* deflect some of the pain a vampire will inflict on you with recollections of his past loves. You can change the subject. Talk about the weather, the future of cable TV, the state of the hemline, your oncoming migraine—something that will get him to *stop* for a few minutes. (And that's all it will be, for if Sean Patrick hadn't been rambling on about Serena it would have been Elektra or Cassandra.)

Another tactic you might use is to ask to see a picture of the divine creature he's been making you ill with tales about. He's bound to have a few on hand—on the walls, in the wallet, under the pillow. Ah, you think gazing at the actual images of these creatures of unearthly delight will cause you even greater pain? Don't bet on it.

One vampire guy I'd been dating for about a month used to rave about the spectacular wife who had left him. He threw in all the regulation vampire jive. How they'd taken holidays in St. Bart's and Kitzbühel (meanwhile we're at Pizza Hut); how he'd lavished her with emeralds and blood-red rubies (after he'd suggested we go dutch at Pizza Hut); and because she was "so beautiful, so brilliant," he "could never truly love that way again. Ever." Needless to say, I assumed he had been dumped by someone who looked like Kim Basinger and behaved like Mother Teresa.

Then, one night, back at his apartment, I noticed a photo of a woman taken in what looked like a low-rent Las Vegas motel. I wouldn't say she was plump. Then again, I wouldn't say celebrities like Oprah Winfrey and Delta Burke could do with a little less avoirdupois. That is because, *au fond*, I have a kind nature. But I did suffocate a snort when I asked, "Is *that* your ex?"

"Yeah," he responded softly. "She's a real doll, isn't she?"

If he was referring to those stuffed Miss Piggy toys, then she definitely fit the category of "a real doll." If he was talking about the pretty, porcelain-faced cherubs they sell in places like F.A.O. Schwartz, there's no way she'd ever see a shelf.

She was *fat*. Fat as only women who pour themselves into silver sausage dresses and wear a mop of bleached, electric-shocked hair along with streaks of blue eyeshadow across their lids can be fat.

But to him, she was "a real doll." Vampires, you see, perceive women differently than other men. That's why they're never judges in contests where a balanced judgment is required—like the Miss America Pageant. They see what they *want* to see and are convinced their choices represent a universal ideal. And there's no talking them out of it.

Consequently, had I asked that vampire, "Was that photo taken just minutes before your 'real doll' went into the hospital for life-support liposuction," he would have turned against me and accused me of being petty and jealous. Perhaps he would have been accurate. I guess in my heart, I knew he could never find me—or maybe anyone ever again—quite so lovely.

Forget about my suggestion. Don't ask to see pictures. Even if they prove that all the great loves in his past looked like Quasimodo's homely sisters, you'll never change his gilded memories of what they meant to him.

But here's something you can do. You can take the advice that an old-time sportscaster vampire gave me. He told me that one of the most interesting aspects of his profession was when he and his sportswriter cronies would get together late at night and play "what if." Example: "What if heavyweight fighters Joe Louis and Muhammed Ali had lived in the same time. Who would be the winner in a match between them? And could Mike Tyson have beaten either of them?" Or, "What if Mickey Mantle were playing baseball today. Would his career run as long as Nolan Ryan's?" Or, "What if Joe Namath and Joe Montana were heading equally matched football teams today. Who would prove the better quarterback?"

"Ultimately," the jock vampire told me, "While it was fun to banter about the possibilities, it was an essentially futile exercise. The games—boxing, football, baseball, real life—are always changing. The way people act and react to situations is always changing, and when change intervenes, comparisons are no longer valid."

So it goes with your vampire and the former loves of his life. You are facing him, and the underworld in general, in a way he never could have. That's because you're doing it *now*—and that's a whole new ball game for him.

When you find yourself fidgeting that you're probably not as glamorous as Chloë, as bitingly clever as Adriana, or as feverishly fragile as Ophelia, make a conscious effort to stop the VCR that's running round-the-clock videos of your vampire and his former loves in your brain. Just turn it off. This minute, dammit!

Fighting the ghosts and phantoms of all the loves he's had—and very likely will have—is one of the most frustrating challenges when loving a vampire. You can never win against any of them. But even if you could, they'd never let on. Ghosts, particularly vampire ghosts, don't know how to play fair.

↭ 8 ↭
VAMPIRE ASTROLOGY:
ARE YOU HIS BLOOD TYPE?

 OK. You looked into his eyes, you felt the blood (or what was left of it) rush to your head, and you're sure you've finally found your Prince of Darkness. But is it eternal love or simply blood lust? Could *this* Mr. Bite be *the* Mr. Right? Just what do you really know about this guy, anyway?

Fortunately, the true character of your vampar-amour is readily revealed in his astrological sign. One word of caution here—your vampire may say he was "born" on December 25, but that *doesn't* make him a Capricorn anymore. Rather, you've got to find out the day he became Undead. This takes a lot more savvy than just casually asking to see his passport. (He'll have dozens of passports—all with line drawings, *not*

photos—so you'll never find out that way.) Because vampires are so secretive, you might be inclined to think they were all born (or became Undead) under the signs of Cancer or Scorpio. Don't let that fool you. I've known plenty of Sagittarian vampires. It probably has to do with the holiday season.

So how do you devise ways to get him to reveal his special day? One successful ploy is to harken back to the past. Say he's shown an interest in English history. Bring up the Battle of Trafalgar and ask him what year it took place. If he immediately answers "1805," press it and ask him what day. If he gets all misty-eyed recalling the windy morning of October 21, you've got yourself a vampire who's Undead under Libra—on the cusp with Scorpio!

You may not have the time (or the reference books) to ferret out this type of recondite information. It might be handier for you to use the following "Astrological Guide to the Undead" to find what you're in for should you decide to sink your teeth into this relationship.

(Note: don't despair if you find that your own sign is incompatible with that of your vampire lover's. If the two of you do decide to take the Big Lunge, *you'll* get not only everlasting life, but a brand-new zodiac sign as well! After all, we are talking nothing less than *rebirth* here. Just be sure to plan ahead for the big night. Sure, it takes some of the spontaneity out of the event, but better simpatico than sorry, as they say in Transylvania.)

▼   ▼   ▼

THE ARIES VAMPIRE (MARCH 21-APRIL 19)

Bold, impatient, and headstrong, the Aries vamp lunges at life with lip-smacking gusto. This guy is not one to nibble around the neck, and he's probably already a bit miffed at you for not putting (your throat) out on the first date. (Of course, wise girl, if you'd done *that*, you might not have been around to enjoy a second date!) The Ram Vamp is the most cheerful and optimistic of the zodiac Undead. Truth be told, if *you* thought as highly of yourself as *he* does of himself, you'd be a happy vamper, too. Slightly kinky and heavily into excess, he's been known to indulge in many a *manger à trois*. His boundless enthusiasm does tend to make him accident-prone (he's particularly careless with sharp instruments), but even there his luck persists—after all, red *is* his favorite color, so it makes no difference to him if, by the end of the night, he's covered with it—be it via his marinara sauce or your O positive. Most mortal women find it impossible to resist his sexy "come hither" grin and his uncompromising hunger for anything he can get his teeth into.

The Aries vampire can be a terrific one-night stand if you don't mind looking like death warmed over the next morning, but take my word for it—he's strictly a bite-and-run kind of guy, and his "wham, bam, fang you, ma'am" attitude makes him a poor choice for eternal companionship. For some unfathomable reason, most rock stars are Aries vampires.

▼   ▼   ▼

THE TAURUS VAMPIRE (APRIL 20-MAY 20)
The Bull Vamp is a creature of habit—he was a Taurus before he joined the night shift, and he'll *keep* his sign, thank you very much. He's also one of the more cautious vampires of the zodiac, so don't take it personally if he makes you take at least three blood tests *and* submit to a blind tasting before he'll even consider getting into the clinch with you. Once you have him by the tooth, though, you'll find that he's lethally loyal. His jealousy and possessiveness are legendary—even in a world where possessiveness is king.

Thrifty by nature, you'll often find the Taurus vamp employed as a banker—only instead of T-bills, he's stocking up on type O, which makes him a wonderful choice for the girl who hates to do her own grocery shopping. Tightwad that he is, he *does* display largesse in one area (as if you didn't know!). He will spend eternities making languorous love to you in the safety of his double-combination-locked coffin. And he does it so well, he may even convince *you* that the best things in death are free!

▼   ▼   ▼

THE GEMINI VAMPIRE (MAY 21-JUNE 21)   The Gemini is the butterfly of the zodiac, and your in-

73

tended will often resemble one. A big, black one. A big, black, squeaking, wing-flapping rat of a butterfly—that's the Gemini vamp. This, of course, explains his rather frustrating habit of flitting from one potential meal/mate to the next. Always on the lookout for adventure, *M* words such as monotony, monogamy, and marriage don't even enter into his vocabulary. True, you'll never be bored with this inventive, fun-loving creature, but, like his Aries cousin, the Gemini Undead craves variety too much to settle down (admit it— you didn't really think that was *lipstick* on his collar, did you?), and unless you can figure out a way to keep a different blood type running through each of your major arteries, it's unlikely that you'll convince him to hang around long enough to develop a long-term relationship. He *is* a charmer, and if you're not careful he'll steal your heart along with the requisite pint or so. The problem, however, is that he never seems willing to stick around long enough to *finish you off*, and you'll only end up feeling chronically drained if you pursue him.

▼   ▼   ▼

THE CANCER VAMPIRE (JUNE 22–JULY 21)
This is the guy who always seems to turn up in the movies. You know him—he's the mysterious one, the moody one, the one who loves nothing more than hanging around moonlit cemeteries searching for his one true Vampirella. If you think that angst is sexy, this is the vampire for you, but tread lightly over his

grave. He's extremely sensitive about every little thing under the moon, and when his feelings are wounded he's likely to crawl into his tomb and sulk for centuries. Crab Vamps are sentimental to a fault and are happiest when talking about "the good old days"—like the Renaissance or the Industrial Revolution. His castle will be a cozy pack rat's haven, filled with tattered furniture he'll tell you are antiques and adorned with sweet, embroidered homilies that all read, "A vampire's best (and only) friend is his mother." Should you find your vampire to be a little distant, remember that the way to this one's heart is definitely through his bicuspids, and he'll perk right up if you occasionally present him with a token of your love (sweet young virgins do nicely here). Be prepared to hear a lot about the old bats who have done him wrong in the past—he can hold a grudge *forever*. Just smile sweetly, offer him a fresh Bloody Mary, and take comfort in the fact that, like everything else he's acquired in life (and after), he'll *never* give you up.

▼   ▼   ▼

THE LEO VAMPIRE (JULY 22-AUGUST 22)
Having the sun as a planetary ruler is not an easy thing for the Leo vampire, who of course can never get out into the daylight, but he's managed to make do rather nicely with a UV-intensive tanning bed as a coffin (George Hamilton only *says* he gets his golden glow on the Riviera). Leo vamps are the dramatists of the Undead, and this, combined with their fierce appe-

tite for immediate gratification, can result in a rather overbearing fiend at times. Naturally, his motto is "I vant to suck your blood. *Now*." Once he gets a taste of you he's apt to either split or commit, so if you find him beating his wings against your balcony door soon after your first date, you'll known you're definitely his type (A, B, . . . whatever). Actually, Leo vampires are amazingly easy to please. Just perfect a convincing swoon and play on his love of being first in everything (if you can do it while keeping a straight face, tell him you're a virgin), and you'll soon have him chomping at the bit for a serious relationship.

An enamored Leo makes for a potentially great romance, but if you'd rather he take his teeth elsewhere, you'd better have a very large cross handy, and you'd better be prepared to hit him over the head with it. Leos, especially those of the underworld variety, simply refuse to take hints.

▼▼   ▼▼   ▼▼

THE VIRGO VAMPIRE (AUGUST 23–SEPTEMBER 22)   You need only one thing to win the heart of the Virgin Vampire. Alas, that one thing is *perfection*! As the crème de la crème of the underworld (that's what *he* considers himself, anyway—and, very probably, you do too), he can be discriminating to a fault. Most Virgo vamps will even go so far as to accept only a woman whose type is AAA plus! (Don't fret too much about that though. You can always get a doctor to forge a certificate. The Virgo vamp is discriminating. He's

76

not a detective.) Once you have him in your web, you'll find you have a true patrician who simply adores spending nights at romantic formal dinners and black tie-affairs, and shopping the midnight sales at Ralph Lauren boutiques. (Ralph, aside from being a Virgo himself, was of course the one who brought back the western look, complete with all those perky red bandannas tied around the throat.) Unfortunately, Virgo is a bit of a hypochondriac, and much of your time will be spent reassuring this paragon of the underworld that he's not going to die if he catches a cold (he's already dead, remember?) Once you've made his problems yours, you can look forward to an eternity of perfection, which is very nice if you aspire to becoming the Madonna (the saint, not the singer) of the night world. If not, you'd better consider moving on to a new castle and finding a vampire who's not quite so concerned about your rating with the local blood bank.

▼▼   ▼▼   ▼▼

THE LIBRA VAMPIRE (SEPTEMBER 23-OCTOBER 23) How can you spot an Undead Libra? He's the one thrashing around his luxurious designer coffin in the middle of the afternoon trying to decide whether to wear the Armani or the Valentino dinner jacket under his cape that night! This vampire may be indecisive, but once he's made the commitment to being Undead, he's going to go down looking his best. Libra vamps are suckers (ah, so to speak) for elegance and beauty. You, dear girl, must therefore always be sure to look stylish (even if it means you have to shoplift to do it) so he'll think you can afford the extensive late-night shopping trips he needs to stir him from his occasional periods of withdrawal. A master of giving (and accepting) compliments as well as hickeys, the Libra Undead has been called the diplomat of the living dead. Alas, his extravagance is offset by his chronic inability to make ends meet, so don't get the idea you're going to be able to lie around the coffin all day eating bonbons and perfecting your lily-white makeup technique. This vampire needs to be *taken care of*. If you have a degree in nursing, psychotherapy, or Swedish massage, go after this October guy. He's got all the time in the world to be coddled, and he'll be forever in your embrace if you take the upper hand in the relationship. As one Libra vamp told me, your October guy *lives* (well, sort of) for the day he can say "at last, someone is biting *my* neck!"

▼   ▼   ▼

THE SCORPIO VAMPIRE (OCTOBER 24-NO-VEMBER 21) Being Undead under Scorpio is an awesome responsibility because it's the sign people *expect* a vampire to be "born" under—what with Halloween and everything. Because of their mythic charisma, however, Scorpio vamps are able to rise from the tomb—and just about everywhere else—to the occasion. They know all the mojo about love and sex (which they think is the same thing), have more than a passing interest in the occult, excel in arts like hypnosis, and basically are satisfied when they can control and dominate anything and everything that comes their way. Black is the Scorpio vamp's favorite color, so wear it to death! Oh, and let me add that they are insanely jealous! What else could you ask from a vampire? Although profoundly passionate, Scorpio vamps are not easy to get into the clinch. They would rather spend nights home alone than waste their sharp intellects and incisors on a woman they don't think is up (or down) to their level.

As far as the zodiac underworld goes, though, the Scorpio vamp is close to ideal. He's compelling, smolderingly sexy, and absolutely evil. But be warned: forget the casual fling if you find yourself playing footsies with a November Undead. He *does* take prisoners.

▼   ▼   ▼

THE SAGITTARIUS UNDEAD (NOVEMBER 22– DECEMBER 21) Here's the party vampire of the zodiac. This guy is such a lively ball of fire, it'll take you some time to even *realize* he's Undead. He's also one of the hardest to keep track of—he's never in the same coffin for two nights running. The reason the Archer Vamp is always on the move is that his blunt outspokenness (which he'll call "honesty") has caused him to tread on so many toes, he's burnt all his bridges behind him. He's so "alive" with enthusiasm, you may wonder, "Haven't you *learned* anything all these years?" He hasn't. No matter what's happened to his teeth, the heart of the Sag Vamp remains that of a lad's, and all you have to do to keep this prize is to laugh at his silly knock-knock jokes, pay his gambling debts, put up with his philandering, and smile at his sincerity when he tells you you've put on some weight. The scatter-brained Sag Undead's "life" (or what he recalls of it) has been littered with broken dates and warmed-over TV dinners. If you can keep up with his fast-thinking philosophical mind, you are probably taking more methamphetamine than is good for you.

▼   ▼   ▼

THE CAPRICORN UNDEAD (DECEMBER 22-JANUARY 19)   Many a Capricorn chooses to become Undead under the same sign—not because, like the Taurus vampire, these guys dislike change per se, but because Capricorns see vampirism as a guarantee that "you *can* take it with you!" Before even nuzzling your neck, the Goat Vamp will try to excite you by telling you how much money he's made—and how he intends to keep it. Capricorns don't care so much about what you wear or how you fix your hair—just show up at his tomb some night (it'll always be in the posh, high-rent area of the cemetery) with your Dun and Bradstreet, an attorney, a CPA, and a willingness to turn over all your worldly possessions and you'll have him for life. *Your* life, that is. The most upwardly mobile in the Realm of the Undead, the Cap Vamp's little black book is a printout of the most rich and famous women of the last few centuries—heiresses he knew could give him a leg up in the netherworld. And on the subject of "nether," once that goat's got what *he* wants, he will get very *down* to your particular erotic tastes. "A fair exchange is no robbery" is the goat's maxim. Although he's looking for background and breeding in the woman who will be this century's Vampirella, he will be reluctant to divulge anything about *his* past. Frankly, you're better off not knowing. Just like an insider trader can juggle junk bonds and futures, the Goat Vamp can negotiate time, cash, and space—which is why he's been able to hang onto those devilishly boyish looks for such a very long time.

▼   ▼   ▼

THE AQUARIUS UNDEAD (JANUARY 20-FEBRUARY 19)   The Water-Bearer Vampire is an outgoing nonconformist who will dazzle you with his far-out, freewheeling philosophies. Unpossessive and "cool," this hipster-type vamp wants to be everybody's friend—including the women he necks with, promises to take out on the following Saturday night, and then doesn't call. But he doesn't *mean* to hurt anybody. His mind is so filled with "big" thoughts that encompass the entire underworld, he can't concentrate on just one neck. His preoccupation with sex, drugs, and rock & roll have taken their toll over the years, and you'll be tempted to bring him back to glowing health by serving up warm, tasty hemoglobin soups, knitting him toasty wool socks, and creating a warm and cheery crypt. It might take him a century or more to notice you're even around—but, honestly, would you want that free spirit any other way?

▼   ▼   ▼

THE PISCES UNDEAD (FEBRUARY 20-MARCH 20)   It's been said by various vampire astrologers that the Fish Undead are the sexual degenerates of the Vampire Zodiac. Of course, they have some bad qualities too. Physically irresistible, the Pisces vamp is the fast-talking salesman of the underworld who'll lure you into his dark, inviting, and spookily unfamiliar atmosphere. Swept away in his world of grand illusion, you'll give yourself totally to him. And before long, you'll find yourself running his ordinary errands. The Fish Undead has an uncanny way of making you do things you'd never dreamed of—fantasized about, maybe, but never, ever *dreamed*. He is poetic and intense, and many a psychic vampire is Undead under this sign. His keen intuition will ferret out even your most hidden secrets—like the location of your credit cards, checkbook, and other negotiables. He is a master of disguise—you may not even recognize him when he's out with your best friend or younger sister. Fish Undead regale their ladies with gifts of expensive perfume. That's because it contains alcohol, which they love to smell and taste on a fair maiden's neck! If you're looking for a codependent vampire, look no further than the fish.

❧ 9 ❧
THOSE VAMPIRE QUIRKS
THAT DRIVE WOMEN CRAZY

 We women are willing to accept that vampires are total charmers, but let's face it, they have some *fatal* flaws. A glaring one is that they always want things *their* way!

For instance, one summer night near Paris's Pere-Lachaise, I met Jean-Loup, whom I suspected at once to be a vampire. How? Well, aside from the fact that we'd met in a famous cemetery, he had an *all-too-intimate* knowledge of the workings of the Court of Versailles *and* he'd eighty-sixed my suggestion to go to a bistro and split an order of escargot. But then he surprised me. He made a date for *dawn* at the Gare du Nord, offering to book a *wagon-lit* and take me to the south of France. *Quel* fun! But the experience turned out to be *un grand* bummer. If you've ever been in one of those snug little couchettes with the window shades drawn, you know it feels like the dead of night and you've been laid out in one of those you-know-whats.

Jean-Loup was having the time of his life (or whatever he referred to it as), but I was getting a royal pain in the neck as well as other parts of my anatomy. There I was in La Belle France with no scenery, no room service, no nothing!

I made my bitter disappointment clear and that night at dinner in the Hotel Carlton in Cannes, Jean-Loup tried to make it up to me over bottles of Veuve Cliquot rosé—my fave bubbly. Alas, he was only trying to soften me up for the news that he'd planned for us to make the *return* trip to Paris as dawn came up on La Croisette. I was adamant and told him, "No way, José." My attitude hurt and angered him. Vampires are notoriously thin-skinned, but I was able to turn him around to my way of thinking by fiddling with the cameo hanging from the slenderest red ribbon of a choker necklace he'd brought along for the ride. The bottom line was that I got a day at the beach while Jean-Loup slept in, and the following night we *drove* back to Paris in the comfort of a luxurious, big, black limo he'd rented.

The "wanting their own way" extends to sex, travel, conversation, where to sit, what to order, and what to watch on TV. This can be very frustrating to the new vampire girl, but once you understand that his arrogant, volatile, dominating personality is couched in a mysterious interpretation of passive-aggressive behavior, you will find it more acceptable. At least that's what made it easier for me to deal with Philippe of Toulouse, another French vampire in my past.

It was on our third weekend together that Philippe took me to a tony restaurant. Granted, my big, brown eyes may have been dripping semisweet chocolate messages *d'amour* his way, but I honestly believed I was playing my romantic cards close to the vest.

Over emerald Chartreuse and out of the clear, midnight-blue sky, Philippe sharply announced, "You know this affair of ours isn't going to go on forever." (To my mind, it wasn't even going to go on that much longer in the here and now!)

He then went on to tell me that he had no intention of falling in love with me or "getting involved." He continued hurting my feelings and wounding my pride in his lilting singsong French, assuring me that he wanted whatever it was we had to be "honest." "Honest" to him meant that our relationship was a *divertissement* and I shouldn't get my hopes up that any antique engagement rings would be flashing my way in the future—of which he had plenty more than I did. (Rings *and* future.)

Philippe was using the timeworn "put her in her place with cruel honesty" vampire gambit to beat down my spirits. Ploys like this are one of the reasons vampires can claim, "I have never struck a woman in my life." As if they needed to lift a finger to drop you to the floor!

But did I cry, grovel, beg, or plead with him to reconsider his pronouncement on the brief life span of *nous*? Not then and there, I'm proud to say!

Rather, I retaliated with, "Listen, Philippe, Toulouse has some lovely, lively cemeteries with gorgeous posies [it *is* the violet capital of France, you know], but for me, it's not exactly the garden spot of the world. And, *mon vieux*, I think you should know here and now that I am relegating you to the tiniest footnote in my "*roman d'amour!*"

With that, I hailed the server for the check and Philippe changed his attitude. He started nibbling my hand and cooing, "Ah, *cherie*, I'm so glad we are of the same mind. Now we can have our nice little affair with none of the stupid expectations!"

His unexplained reaction led me to spend the next several weeks wondering what Philippe *really* meant by that cryptic remark. Was he:

1. Falling in love with my fiercely independent spirit and planning to gradually move our relationship onto a more serious plateau?
2. Being on the level and sincerely relieved he had a girlfriend he didn't have to even *pretend* any long-term interest in?

Since Number Two was *not* an acceptable answer to me (or any other vampire aficionada), I chose to believe in Number One and stopped to smell the violets until Philippe proved to be another dead-end affair.

Yet another irritating vampire quirk is their

spongelike ability to freeload. One spring I was covering an Italian wine festival in the wistfully fragrant city of Verona (where classic vampire lovers Romeo and Juliet called it a day). On the Alitalia night flight over, I was sitting next to Julian, a sabre-toothed dreamboat who was witty, outgoing, and debonair.

Even before the movie came on, he had discovered the name of my hotel and established how long I would be staying there. All he told me about his schedule was that his plans were "vague," but "if it's convenient for you, I'd like for us to get together in Verona."

In reality, it was far more convenient for *him*. He crashed at my hotel, and, since I was occupied with tasting Chianti and Pinot Grigio during the day, I got to see very little of him. By the time I'd return in the evening, he'd already left for his nocturnal *passagiata* through town.

Julian's presence (or nonpresence, as the case was) made it extremely difficult for me to have any sort of decent social life during the festival because he had pawned himself off to the concierge as my *fidanzato*. Some fiancé! He never even bought me a plate of pasta. He did show *some* style, though. The laundry, phone, and drinks charges he signed to my account were not outrageous. Good thing he didn't know I keep my credit cards under my Water-Pik!

One of the most unforgivable vampire quirks that afflicts women is the way they are always setting themselves up as a "challenge"—a challenge we can't seem to resist. One of my best friends, an architect named Camille, has had a long history of vampire lovers.

87

They *all* presented her with a challenge she was compelled to accept. Like many vampire gals, she feels True Love comes with a high-risk obstacle course. Since I've known her, she's been involved with a (married) Finnish poet; a (married) mobster; a (married) out-of-work drummer; and a (married but sexually ambivalent) dentist. Finally, she met the Right Vampire. Mr. Perfect Teeth was married, too, but had the added cachet of having formerly been a priest. He was the father of three children under the age of four and hopelessly torn between his responsibilities to "God and man." According to Camille, he was also great in the sack.

Camille spent four of the best years of her life meeting the "challenge" this vampire presented. She gave up the chase when he skedaddled somewhere north of Nova Scotia, leaving behind her, the wife, and *five* kids.

Therapists who have treated vampire victims suggest that when confronted with the uncontrollable need to pick up the challenge put forth by a vampire, they take the energy they are bound to expend and channel it into other, more sensible, endeavors like Formula One racing, training for the Olympic luge team, swimming the English Channel (both ways), and solving the problem of world hunger. Therapists realize that achieving those sorts of feats won't have the same kick as taking on the challenge of making a gadabout vampire sink his teeth into a real relationship with you — but they can be equally exhausting.

Enough of the trivial quirks any real woman can

adjust to in living with her vampire. Let's get to the issue that has us climbing the walls. That is: WHY IS SEX WITH A VAMPIRE SO MUCH BETTER THAN IT IS WITH A REGULAR GUY??????????

One night at a Vampire Victims support group session this question came up, and I'd like to share with you some of the responses a handful of the participants came up with.

- ▼ *Michelle, 28, pharmacist*: "Vampires never say dumb things like, 'Was it good for you?' They know how good it was for you!" (And probably wouldn't care if it wasn't.)
- ▼ *Sharon, 31, dental hygienist*: "A vampire makes a sensual production of undressing you. He never fumbles around. He always know just where the J-spot is." (He's had years of practice, remember?)
- ▼ *Valerie, 26, TV production assistant*: "A vampire wants to know all your sexual fantasies. And then he'll act them out with you!" (Sure, and use them against you somewhere down the line.)
- ▼ *Christine, 30, advertising copywriter*:

"Vampires aren't afraid to let go in bed. They sweep you away with their passion. You find yourself saying, doing things you never *dreamed* of before. They know how to get down and dirty!" (Look where they're coming from!)

▼ *Hilary, 27, sous-chef*: "What makes a vampire great in bed is the same thing that makes him great *out* of bed. He knows how to *listen*. In bed, though, he's listening to what your body is telling him. Yeah, that's what it is. He can carry on a conversation with your body." (That's because you've already gone brain dead and it's all he has to talk to!)

▼ *Barbara, 24, receptionist*: "He's tuned into you. He has no agenda of what *he* thinks sex should be like. You know, ten minutes for mesmerizing, five minutes for swooning, and then three hours for neck mauling. He knows how to go with the flow." (And he's got all the time in the world to do it.)

▼ *Jan, 35, sales representative*: "Vampires can put a woman's pleasure first. They know how to play you like a violin, and they always know they're going to get what *they* want eventually!" (And what they want will all be on tape in the hidden videocam.)

Melanie, a 29-year-old botanist, offered a more complex analysis of what makes vampire sex better than "regular" sex. She said, "It's the way he's able to mess up your emotions. Making love to a vampire can bring back the remembrance of every hurt you ever felt from the time you didn't get a valentine in the second grade to two nights ago when he said he'd call and didn't. The vampire makes you believe that he can kiss all those hurts away and that you'll always be safe in his arms. Yet, other times, sex with a vampire can get so crazy-intense you need to keep a paper bag on the night table in case you start hyperventilating. Then there are the *most* magical times when the feelings between you become so fragile, so bittersweet, so achingly perfect, you think, 'This is so wonderful, I don't care if it's the last time!' "

Eventually, you know, there probably *will* be a last time.

✤ 10 ✤
TAKING THE BIG LUNGE: ARE YOU READY FOR COMMITMENT?

One of the big attractions of a vampire guy is that, unlike so many of today's men, he isn't afraid or unwilling to make a commitment.

Commitment, *marriage*, is a crucial element in a relationship with a vampire—but perhaps I should explain how vampires define *commitment*, as it was explained to me one night in Estoril, a seaside resort outside Lisbon.

I was having dinner with a Portuguese vampire named Antonio, whom I'd met through a stateside acquaintance in the travel industry. Antonio's opening line to me was pure vampire puff: "Chris [the acquaintance] told me about you—but he didn't mention you had the most beautiful neck in all of Europe!" I guess that's because Chris wasn't a vampire and would be embarrassed to lard a woman with that sort of cheesy flattery.

Antonio had an important job in the airline industry. At least that's what I assumed, because he was always flying through the air with the greatest of ease. He was tall, sleek, saturnine, and fluent in eight languages. Over a bottle of *vinho verde* and steamy plates of clams and pork—a tasty dish no other country seems to know about—he remarked, "Married? My *wife* is married, *I* am not."

Since I wasn't planning to spend an eternity in Lisbon and Antonio was too self-assured a vampire to truly capture my fancy (I prefer the type who needs me to *save* him), I could accept his cavalier attitude toward "for keeps" and enjoy our alliance for its casually continental charm.

But suppose I had fallen into his web! Suppose I had sunk into the morass and mire of thinking I was in love with him and it would last forever! Suppose I had been awed by the glamour and romance of sipping Madeira in back-street cafés and decided to give up my happy home life to become a miserable, black-shawled fado singer—or whatever happens to American girls when they lose their hearts, minds, and traveler's checks to Iberian vampires? And suppose, after a couple of months of having Antonio as the husband/lover/father/brother vampires tend to become to a woman, I became disenchanted and wanted the *big out*! How could I escape having kissed my real life good-bye after pledging my troth to a vampire?! I'd be in the proverbial kettle of fish without a paddle, wouldn't I?

So many lovely, intelligent women I know have found themselves in that awkward situation. They meet a vampire, become bedazzled, and rush into making a rash commitment that they later ruefully regret.

Because I know how easy it is to want to declare, "Yes! Now! *Forever!*" to a vampire almost from the get-go, I've devised a little quiz that should help you gauge your true feelings and determine whether you've crossed that tiny gap between fascination and love. It will help you decide whether you're only in for the fling or are prepared to go the distance with your vampire.

OK. Pencils out! And remember, no cheating!

Are You Ready for Vampire Matrimony?

1. It is the morning of your birthday. Your idea of a great celebration would be to:

    A. Go on an unlimited shopping spree on Rodeo Drive.

    B. Jump on a plane to Perth to keep a date with Mel Gibson.

C. Win a landmark legal decision for a cause you're passionately devoted to.

D. Kick over some dead flowers and crawl into a coffin with your special guy.

2. *You've gotten a tremendous promotion and are given a choice of perks to go with it. You insist on:*

A. A stock-option clause plus pension plan plus unlimited expenses for travel, entertainment, and whatever else your little heart desires.

B. A designer-decorated office and a male secretary whose only credentials are that he looks like John Kennedy, Jr. Better still, he *is* John Kennedy, Jr.

C. Your entire staff devoting 10 percent of the work week to doing some form of volunteer work, which the company will pay for.

D. Coming in at 7:00 A.M., skipping lunches and coffee breaks, and even working weekends so long as you *never* have to work nights.

3. *You have won a fabulous vacation for two and are able to take your vampire guy anywhere in the world. Your holiday choice is:*

A. A bank tour of Switzerland where you get to open your own unnumbered passbook account.

B. The beaches of French Polynesia where you'll sexily smolder in the sunshine.

C. A Help World Hunger trip to Africa with Audrey Hepburn. You always loved her in *Mary Poppins* (or whoever it was in *Mary Poppins*).

D. A one-day/six-night trip to Transylvania. You hear the cuisine is unspeakable.

4. *You are walking down the street and find a bundle of small bills totaling $524. Your first instinct is to:*

A. Call your broker to have him add a little something to your mutual fund.

B. Treat yourself to an expensive lunch complete with a round for the bar.

C. Ask passersby if anyone recently dropped some money. You never know, whoever lost it might still be in the area.

D. Buy him the black silk cape he'd admired but you couldn't afford until this very minute.

5. *Your high school reunion is coming up and you want to take your vampire. He nastily declines because he thinks anything to do with your past is trivial. You:*

A. Rent a chauffeured limousine for the night and go by yourself—dressed to kill.

B. Pick up the cutest guy at the biker or stockbroker bar the night of the event and drag him along.

C. Go alone, explaining your boyfriend "just doesn't go in for these kinds of things."

D. Go alone but lie about the "important" engagement your boyfriend has that prevents his being with you. Then slink back to him, apologizing profusely for having gone in the first place.

6. *Your vampire tells you he's "going out of town on business for a few days." You know he's lying and suspect he might be giving you the good-bye look. You immediately:*

A. Go out on the town and amuse yourself by catching some shows, trying out new restaurants, and buying some clothes, all of which you use his credit card to do.

B. Tart yourself up and head for the singles bars and discos. You know the old adage, "In the dark, all vampires look the same!"

C. Use the free time to do important things like clean the kitchen, volunteer at the local library, finally learn to program your VCR. You remain calm because you are convinced, "If it's meant to be, it will be."

D. Tie one on and have a refreshing crying jag, which galvanizes you into action. You tap into his answering machine and secretly follow him as he nightly wanders from his crypt.

7. *At his crypt one night, he serves you wine and cheese from a platter upon*

which is painted a formidable Madonna and child. Knowing a bit about art, you appreciate its value. You:

A. Ask to "borrow" it for a brunch you're giving. You know you can get a forger friend to make up a copy you'll give back to him later.

B. Comment on the remarkable likeness between you and the Madonna.

C. Quietly suggest that spilling Corton Charlemagne and Camembert on an Old Master does nothing for its patina so perhaps he'd best store the nice platter somewhere safe.

D. Gaze at him knowingly, stub your cigarette into the painting, and comment, "I always thought Tintoretto was a real zero, too."

8. *You and a girlfriend are seeing* Phantom of the Opera *for the eighth time. During intermission, you spot your vampire at the lobby bar with another woman. You:*

A. Check out what she's wearing. If her frock is off the rack and her pearls are paste, you know he won't be around her for long!

B. Dump your girlfriend, pick up the good-looking usher, and introduce him to your vampire as your date.

C. Make polite introductions and enjoy the second act. After all, you still keep telling yourself, "If it's meant to be . . ."

D. Push yourself toward them, begin gasping for breath, and, while holding onto her hair to give you support, slump to the floor, audibly whispering, "I'm pregnant."

9. *Your vampire has asked you to meet him at London's swank Ritz Hotel for a Jack-the-Ripper festival. You don't have the money for airfare or suite, much less the quaint Victorian costume he wants you to wear to it. You:*

A. Tell him if he wants you there, he'll have to spring for the fare, the room, *and* the outfit.

B. Call the airline pilot you've been seeing on the side and have him arrange emergency transport with the claim that you're his sister and have got to care for an ailing auntie in Ealing.

C. Decline with regrets. "If it's meant to be . . ."

D. Do *anything*! Rifle through your aged grandma's purse for loose change, tell the office manager you need an advance on your salary for your brother's sex change operation, kite a check, hold up a convenience store! You *will* be by his side!

10. *It's 12:06 A.M., New Year's Day. Your vampire did not show up for your New Year's Eve date as he had sworn he would. You:*

A. Hastily cover the caviar in plastic wrap and put the Champers back in the fridge. No sense letting it go to waste.

B. Go out to the noisiest Greek restaurant in town. There will be plenty of music, high spirits, souvlaki, ouzo, and vampires to get you through the night.

C. Make a list of resolutions you can stick to before turning in.

D. Frantically call the police and hospitals to find out what happened to him (as if *they'd* know, you silly twit) before seriously considering slashing your wrists.

OK, it's time to check your answers.

If most of them are *A*, I'm afraid you're far too much the material girl to be a vampire bride. Your values are all wrong for a man who's been through the bad and good times he has. Actually, your values are all wrong, period. My advice is: go out with as many vampires as you like, but keep your fancy free.

If most of your responses fell into the *B* category, I can safely say you'd be courting disaster if you made a lifelong (or whatever they're calling it now) commitment to a vampire. You're far too fickle, far too filled with élan vital (nearly as fatal as a stake in the heart to a vampire) to make it last a week, much less an eternity. Just ask Fergie.

Now, if most of your answers were in the *C* group, you're just what a vampire is looking for. You're too good to be true, and think of all the fun he'll have corrupting you! But how will you feel about your fall from grace a century down the road? And will he grow tired of your treacly Pollyanna, do-gooder, jejune qualities before long? And what happens when your sweetness has tarnished? There are a lot of gray areas in this sort of vampire relationship, but, as you said yourself, "If it's meant to be . . ."

Now, my little friend, if the majority of your responses were *D* you know as well as I do that you're ready to take the Big Lunge! If you hear of any boutiques that are having sales on little black dresses, you might as well make the investment and stock up now. You're going to be having some very long nights ahead of you. Good luck!

❦ 11 ❦
THE FUTURE AND YOUR VAMPIRE

The good news about saying "forever" to a vampire is knowing you have the security of a stable relationship. Nothing will change. He'll always be floating about somewhere in your life, demanding your attention, draining your energy, and causing you grief over what he's been up to all night. The bad news is also the same. *Nothing* will change. But hey, if you can live with that sort of death sentence, who's to criticize your choice! You should know a few more specifics about what your future holds, however.

While most relationships have their ups and downs, life with a vampire has Grand Canyon chasms. No emotional or moral disagreement, no petty dispute will ever be considered so "trivial" that "sleeping on it" becomes an option. He'll keep you up all night over the merits of type A over type B with a ham sandwich! But it's always worth putting in the time. Those pre-dawn, making-up necking sessions can get awfully scrumptious!

If you have a normal nine-to-five job, this means you'll be averaging (tops) two to three hours sleep per night. Don't let this daunt you. Many vampire brides have told me that, through meditation and dangerous prescription drugs, they have been able to keep up with their vampire's schedule. Some, unfortunately, have reported suffering side effects such as contracting lockjaw from constant yawning and sustaining broken arms and ankles from falling down with exhaustion. Flu and cold symptoms also tend to plague the vampire gal—no matter how many iron-rich vitamins she takes.

Besides Chronic Fatigue Syndrome and its related maladies, a long-term relationship with a vampire can also play havoc with your weight. I scientifically proved the amazing connection between vampire separation and chocolate binging when I was dating Freddy, a vampire from another part of the world. (Well, they're all from another part of the world, but this one lived in a charming Agatha Christie–type village outside London. London is a favorite vampire town. There are even special Underground trains that only stop at their stations.)

Because ours was a long-distance romance, we didn't have the luxury of simple dating. You know, the kind where you get picked up and dropped off after a certain reasonable amount of time has elapsed. Instead, whenever we wanted to get together, distance forced us to stick it out for a couple of endless days and all-too-brief nights. Here's where the chocolate comes in.

Every time I had to say cheery-bye to Freddy, leaving him in a dark room, snugly tucked under the duvet in some smart hotel (Freddy was one of my more *sportif* vamps), I could hardly make it to the lobby without desperately wanting a chocolate candy bar. And I'm not even fond of chocolate! Even Freddy knew that, because he always gobbled the foil-wrapped goody on *my* pillow as well as the one the housekeeper had left on his. (Then again, he probably would have done that even if he thought I was dying for a chokkie. Vampires can get so picayune over little things like candy.)

The minute I knew I would be separated from Freddy for any length of time, my body would begin to rage in a chocolate fever. In predawn airport lounges I scrambled for the change that would release Three Musketeers and Mars bars from their vending-machine prisons. When Freddy would leave me in *my* corner of the world, I was able to get hold of the ritzier Neuhaus variety to subdue my frenzy.

After several vampire holidays followed by chocolate binges (followed by guilt and self-loathing), I went to see a nutritionist friend who specializes in vampire appetites. She explained the phenomenon. Chocolate is high in a chemical called phenylethylamine, which some medical researchers believe is produced irregularly by people who suffer depression from unrequited love. Since I was aware that I was just another petal in

Freddy's daisy chain of blondes, I was indeed suffering and needed all the phenylethylamine I could get to help make it through the day.

Even the most permanent relationships with a vampire require long periods of separation, so a vampire bride-to-be has to consider the unwanted calories she's going to accumulate in an effort to fill the void he's left in her rapidly deteriorating life. And that's just the beginning.

If you're thinking you can make a lifelong commitment to a vampire *and* have a successful career, you're whistling in the dark. It's not that your vampire will *actively* discourage you from pursuing your dreams. On the contrary—your accomplishments make him *proud*. I've heard many a vampire crow to his cronies, "My wife is a brilliant viola da gamba player/prosecuting attorney/dedicated veterinarian" (you can fill in the achievement of choice). But then they invariably add, "But she's put that aside *for now*." And, tootsie, you better know that "for now" means *forever!* Yet he won't be the one to force you into a professional abyss. *You'll* be the one to cry uncle because your vampire—with no verbal demands whatsoever—will make it impossible for you to stretch yourself to the limits you haven't even imagined yet.

Half your day, remember, will go into planning what to wear for your vampire that night. Throw in a couple of hours checking out the candy stores for the chocolate fix you'll be needing, and before you know it, there's only 10 hours left for the weeping and gnashing of teeth that are such a momentous part of vampire love.

You know how the story goes. You've been married, engaged, or "living" with a vampire for a reasonable amount of time—say, three years. In three years a trust, an understanding, a sense of well-being and reliability should have developed between the two of you as it does in normal male-female relationships. It hasn't. Every time he's late for an appointment or hasn't materialized when he said he would, you *cannot* sit there and tell yourself, "He's probably tied up in a traffic jam or just lost track of time." No sir. You push every last one of your mental panic buttons and invent gruesome scenes to explain his absence. You see him lying by the side of some deserted road with a stake in his heart; you imagine the night plane he's on has run into an air pocket and will be forced to circle the ground until the dangerous dawn; you envision his being mugged by a gang of vampire bashers and left in a pool of blood by the city dump. Then you figure out he's met another woman who's caught his eye and the horrors begin in earnest!

So, instead of getting on with practicing a Bach fugue, going over a brief for a case you're trying, or doing something as necessary and mundane as the laundry, you hit the phone and start calling your friends. Not your *real* friends. They're sick and tired of your vampire bellyaching. You call the other vampire wives with whom you've commiserated about *their* vampire problems because you figure they owe you. You go over all the absurd possibilities searching for clues, and by the time he finally slinks through the door, you're a blubbery bundle of nerves and so grateful to see him you don't even have the temerity to ask where the hell he's been.

And if he did tell you, you'd waste another handful of days wondering what he really meant.

Nothing a vampire tells you can be taken "as is." Like the night Freddy and I were at this schmaltzy Hungarian restaurant. (Next time a vampire takes you to one of these hot spots, check to see how many times the violinist strikes up "Dark Eyes." They play it whenever a vampire walks into the room—it's like the "Hail to the Chief" of the underworld.)

Freddy was being particularly gallant that night, paying me so many tender compliments I felt like butter in the sun. I hardly put a dent in my blini. After a few snifters of Armagnac, we returned to our hotel about 2:00 A.M.

Freddy took me in his arms and nuzzled, "You know what's so wonderful about being with you? I can *talk* to you. Getting a little neck isn't all that important. With so many women, you try to hurry them through their dinner so you can get to *your* dinner as quickly as possible."

Because I was still fairly new to vampire love back in the Freddy era, I simpered to myself, "Hm, maybe this is getting *serious*." After rehashing the story with several of my more experienced colleagues, however, I got the true picture of what Freddy's honeyed words were hiding: Freddy thought I was a delightful little chatterbox, but I wasn't ringing any of his bells. So he'd talk with me until he was blue in the face, then we'd go back to our hotel where he'd hold me in his arms until he could see the little REM fluttering behind my lids (he'd probably doctored the brandy!). *Then*, he'd creep downstairs and have a blissfully unenlightened bite with some swan-necked barmaid with the IQ of a newt! *Then* he'd slide back into bed with me! Since I expected him to sleep in all day, I'd wake up, hit the hotel health club, go shopping or sightseeing, and not suspect a thing. Oh, the beast!

It just goes to show you that nothing a vampire says, from "My, your hair looks nice today" to "I think the pet raven has developed a cough," can be taken at face value. It must be dissected, probed, recast in a million facets of light, translated into lost cultural idioms, and then played back over and *over* again. That takes far more time than it does to establish a meaningful profession.

Before too long, you'll get used to taking your place in the professional failure chain. You won't mind being passed over for promotions or being smartly informed to "shape up or ship out" by your superiors, and in time a comfortable lethargy should take over 90 percent of your will power. Some vampire wives often find other careers more compatible with their lifestyles, like substitute teaching, toll collecting, parttime treasure hunting, and runway modeling.

More aggressive vampire mates apply for welfare and government giveaways to help pay the bills. Because many vampire gals feel that they were "born lucky" (and who's to argue!), they also invest their time and money in state lotteries, slot machines, and bingo games, hoping against hope for the Big Hit.

Having a Baby Dracula is something every dewy-eyed vampire bride dreams of. Nothing is more cuddly and adorable than a wee little vamp, biting on a bottle and playing innocent, childish games with cockroaches, toads, and bats.

An immutable law of nature (in the event you weren't aware of it) is: when a real woman has a child with a vampire, the baby's personality will be just like the father's. So you can expect your offspring to be demanding, petulant, obstreperous, unpredictable, often unintelligible, narrow-minded, and completely self-absorbed. To add to the baby's charm is that he or she will howl at the moon all the time. But not to worry! You'll have plenty of help raising your little Vlads and Vladettes. Vampires make doting fathers. They love to take the tots hunting and haunting, and will regale vampire babies with thrilling tales of the days and nights of yore. And they actually *look forward* to middle-of-the-night feedings.

While it may not seem so on the surface, sociological surveys have shown that vampire mates have many of the same problems that face corporate wives. There's the upheaval of constant relocation, the separation from long-time friends and family, the isolation of spending so many hours *alone*. Like the corporate wife, the vampire wife (when not gorging on chocolate) will often turn to drink for solace. This is not the sanest or healthiest way of coping, but *sane* and *healthy* are hardly the hallmarks of this kind of relationship, so who am I to cast the first stone?

There is always the possibility that you will land a stay-at-home vampire. That won't guarantee much happiness either. It may cause even more friction in your relationships with your friends and family, because without the added expense of long-distance charges, you'll feel you can call them up all the time! The more you call, the more you're going to have to hear comments like, "We told you not to marry the bum!"

That sort of talk is bound to cause stress in even the most close-knit families, and pretty soon your vampire will refuse to come to your family's gatherings. When your folks express delight that he's a no-show, you'll punish them by not going either. It's a vicious cycle.

As for getting together after work with your friends or maintaining your outside interests—the backgammon league, the Horticultural Society, Citizens for Clean Air, or the Jackson Five—you may as well kiss your membership card good-bye.

While he may not be with you all the time, your vampire will want to be sure you're there for *him*— whenever and wherever he chooses. (He'll sucker you into this way of thinking by singing a few soulful choruses of "Stand by Me" at the appropriate times.) Before too long, he will have taken over your entire being—every breath, every thought, word, and deed. And you'll stay *forever*, because he's convinced you that his need for you is greater than your need for anything—even yourself. Or did *you* convince yourself of that? It gets a little blurry after a while.

✣ 12 ✣
BREAKING UP IS (VERY) HARD TO DO

Somewhere between making a commitment to a vampire and becoming completely drained, you may decide to bail out. It won't be easy. Just like it won't be a piece of cake to jigsaw who and what you were before you met him back together in a hurry. You might even succumb to the temptation of sheepishly returning to his crypt once in a while "for old time's sake." Barring that show of feeblemindedness, you might spend the next decade berating yourself for having squandered all the years, energy, tears, and love (not to mention plasma) in search of the happy ending that never materialized. That's throwing good times after bad. I know this firsthand because, years back, I married a vampire guy.

My vampire, whom I shall call M, was handsome charming, duplicitous, brilliant, poetic, generous, unfaithful, kind, loving, articulate, manipulative, funny, and unpredictable. His addiction to the world of ''spirits'' occasionally caused him to be mortifying. Needless to say, I loved him to distraction. I loved him so much, I wanted to empty myself into him, even if it meant suffocating in the opalescent blue of his eyes.

I knew when we were engaged that, like every vampire, he had a past. My confidence in our perfect future dispelled any healthy concern I might have shown in it. I was so confident, I went so far as to invest in the sort of clothes I'd never worn before. Since I already owned all the vampire gear he went wild for, I began fleshing out my wardrobe with stay-at-home items like organdy dressing gowns I imagined women wore when planning a midnight brunch. I bought Gucci loafers (navy) and the plaid skirt and blazer that went with them to *wear* to the brunch. We would, after all, be part of the vampire Country Club social set, wouldn't we? My career? Oh, perhaps I might knock off the occasional book of children's verse, but most of my time would be spent devoting myself to worthy causes and my vampire.

It began to break down at the wedding, which, you could guess, was an evening affair. M's mother, a dead ringer for Joan Crawford on a bad day, looked at me stonily and said, ''Well, you're a brave soul, taking on all of M's problems. Just don't think the two of you children can come looking to *me* for help.''

''Help? Help for what?'' I wondered. Decorating

was all that came to mind. Like so many vampires, M had a penchant for overembellishment, and his taste ran to the ormolu and chandeliers more appropriate in a bordello in Marseilles than a young professional's apartment.

My honeymoon glow had barely dwindled to a blush when M's problems surfaced. At least *some* of the problems surfaced. They were financial and immense. M made very good money. But it was all spoken for by his previous lives and wives. The monthly payments on the loans he'd taken out were more than most people *earned* in that amount of time. But how was I to have known all this? The expensive presents (like the jewelry I eventually sold to feed the IRS) and splendid dinners (which couldn't be returned) kept me in the dark about his money matters. I hadn't a clue! Or could it have been I wasn't looking for clues? Had you been having the time of your life as I was, you wouldn't have been either.

I dumped the fetching social set clothes in the back of the closet and got a normal job to help pay the greengrocer's and the fishmonger's bills. The job precluded my writing charming children's books or planing brunches, but ready cash always take priority over *Three Little Kittens* and eggs Sardou.

It was a pretty good job, too. The work wasn't very demanding—but in tandem with my vampirish nights, it became a tedious way to make an Undeading.

M loved to stay up late and talk, laugh, drink, meander, and do all those things you'd expect a vampire to do all through the night. Well, of course, he *could*, since he "napped" a significant chunk of the day away on his office couch. That's no doubt why he was able to create this type of 2:00 A.M. scene: it's a spring night. I'm sound asleep. He wakes me up rhapsodizing about it being such a beautiful evening, "we shouldn't let it slip by." Now that I'm slightly roused, he suggests we "take a bottle of champagne [our fridge was always filled with bubbly], stroll to the park [we lived near many city parks], and read poetry [our shelves were filled with every poet from Pliny the Elder to Wilfrid Owen]."

Did I tell him to buzz off? Or that it was a foolish and potentially *dangerous* excursion? Not with those big old blue eyes that held out the secrets of the sea to me, I didn't.

If the truth were told, I'm not entirely sorry I let him Pied Piper me to the point of near-extinction. I was young enough to survive and hang onto all those memories of that lovely man reciting Rupert Brooke in the tipsily grassy near-dawn. But it couldn't last.

It was Renfield who told me about M's affair. Ren (whom we'll call R) and M had gone to school together. R had never married, had never done much of anything but be M's audience and confidant. R told me about the woman. She was an old girlfriend of M's who lived not far from us. He told me M was carrying on with her "for old time's sake." R was nice enough to explain *why* he was letting me in on this agonizing bit of news. He said he:

1. Cared for M.
2. Cared for me almost as much as he cared for M.

115

3. Wanted to see our marriage work because
M *needed* me so much.

Was I stupid or what!?

When M arrived home that night, I had lost every vestige of calm. I was, in fact, screaming and hurling the wedding Baccarat around the living room. I accused him of every misdoing since the Lindbergh kidnapping.

He denied any transgression (surprise, surprise). He admitted, "Of course I know her. Yes, I did go out with her and yes, I even slept with her. But that was then, sweetheart." He followed that with an extraordinary vampire trick. He suggested, "To put your mind at rest, the two of us will walk over to her apartment and she'll tell you point blank that there's *nothing* between us."

He called her to advise her of our visit and led quivery me to meet this cunning little vixen, who smirked, "There's *nothing* between us."

I bought it.

Was I stupid or what?!

Nights like that made mornings at the office a trifle hazy. In fact, I was hazy a major part of the time. Our first Christmas, I was too tired to send cards, too tired to make plans to visit our respective families, and too tired to do anything but shuffle from party to party with him shrieking tidings of comfort and joy.

By New Year's, our little spats had begun in earnest; the making up was growing pathetically frantic.

Even through the cut-velvet fog of vampire love, I could tell I was losing it. By "it" I mean I was losing things like friends, being able to relax with a good book, being able to relax in general. I always felt as though I was coming down with the flu.

I didn't face what was going on directly until it dawned on me that I'd given up my Saturday matinee subscription to the opera. This may not mean much to you, but to *me* those tickets were like ice skates to Katarina Witt; sauté pans to Julia Child; having it all to Helen Gurley Brown. I *love* opera, and I'd been so proud and happy when, after a long wait, I'd gotten my own seat. But I let it go without even thinking because I no longer had the wherewithal, the stamina, the *will* to make it to something as easy to listen to as *L'Elisir D'Amore*.

Of the countless indications that all was not well at *chez moi*, that was the one that scared me into confronting M with the idea of a trial separation.

He did me one better. He insisted we go to a marriage counselor. That's because he knew vampires can get marriage counselors to believe that cruelty is kindness and vice versa. I knew M was winning all the rounds when, after two months, the marriage counselor was telling us that *his* wife had just left him and M began giving *him* comfort and advice. But I kept plugging along because there was a part of me that still hoped the marriage would at least *stabilize*. Instead, the intrigues escalated and the lies lost their grace.

I moved out one snowy day in late January. The Valentine's Day morning after I'd left my vampire, I walked out my door and found the pavement that led the 10 blocks from my house to his dotted with big, red stick-on hearts. (He must have stayed up all night to do that—well, nothing new there.) At my doorstep was a handsome Lalique crystal vase filled with tiny cinnamon hearts. That's the kind of trick vampires will pull when you tell them that under no circumstances do you ever want to see or hear from them again. I suppose they figure that, once you've been bitten, you can get sucked right back into their act.

I had to force myself to be strong enough to remember the *bad* times—the mornings I was too exhausted to go to work; the way I'd let my career, family, friends, interests slip away from me because he was so demanding of my time; those horrible 4:00 A.M. arguments. His *mother* at the wedding!

To be on the safe side, I also made a few crosses from the thorns of wild roses, borrowed a large black dog and painted an extra set of eyes on his forehead with white paint, and spread poppy seeds on the path leading from my place to his—the one he had put the hearts on. That's what I would have done had we been in Transylvania.

Those first weekends alone, I tried to regroup with my family and old pals. I went to movies, gave brunches, listened to Wagner and Puccini, and cried my eyes out. R called several times to see if I would invite him over. He wanted to "come by and see how you're getting along." The sleaze.

Like most vampires, mine didn't graciously give

up the ghost. Since a vampire has all the time in the world to be persuasive, he'll keep you up with 3:00 A.M. phone calls (some of which will elicit a response because you're so damn lonely), send you night-blooming posies, or hire a trio of gypsy violinists to serenade you back into his "life." His persistence is at once his most appealing and most dangerous attribute.

The luxury of having an eternity ahead of him is yet another reason a vampire won't be rushing off to places like the Dominican Republic to get a quickie divorce. In other words, it took as long as we were married to get the papers that made my vampire my ex-vampire.

No, that's not exactly correct. A vampire never becomes an ex. An ex is the kind of guy you might have been in love with, even married to. When it's over, you can look at the photos of the two of you on the beach, on the cruise, at the picnic, and painlessly say, "It was nice while it lasted but we had to get on with our lives." You're even able to absorb the news that he's found happiness with someone else without wanting to vomit. *That's* an ex.

It's different with a vampire. When the flashback slide show of the two of you starts clicking in your memory, you feel a stiletto of regret inserting itself in your left ribcage while the weary lament of "if only" keens in your ears. As time moves on, those little deaths diminish in agony. But they will still be there. And when you hear from a well-meaning friend that he's looking hale and hearty and happy as can be with

ABOUT THE AUTHOR

 Kiki Olson, the author of *A Good Man Is Not Hard to Find*, has dated a bevy of vampires—she was even (briefly) married to one. Between full moons she writes for *Cosmopolitan* and other magazines and is a contributing editor for *New Woman*. In addition, she hosts the radio show "Singles on Saturday" and reviews books for the *New York Times*. Kiki has appeared on "Sally Jessy Raphael," "Donahue," "Geraldo," and "Today." She lives in Philadelphia.